THE NEW PROFESSIONALS

THE NEW PROFESSIONALS
Managing Today's High-Tech Employees

MARY ANN VON GLINOW
University of Southern California

BALLINGER PUBLISHING COMPANY
A Subsidiary of Harper & Row, Publishers, Inc.

International Standard Book Number: 0-88730-271-8

Library of Congress Catalog Card Number: 88-18737

Printed in the United States of America

Library of Congress Cataloging-in-Publication Data

Von Glinow, Mary Ann Young, 1949–
    The new professionals : managing today's high-tech employees /
Mary Ann Von Glinow.
        p.   cm.
    Bibliography: p.
    Includes index.
    ISBN 0-88730-271-8
    1. High technology industries—Personnel management. 2. High
technology industries—Employees. 3. Professional employees.
I. Title.
HF5549.V75   1988
658.3—dc19   88-18737
89 90 91 HC 6 5 4 3 2   CIP

To Steve,
and in Loving Memory of My Mother and C.S.R.

CONTENTS

LIST OF FIGURES

LIST OF TABLES

PREFACE

The New Professionals is designed for managers and researchers concerned with assessing the fit between high-tech firms and the professional employees who work in them. For practicing managers, it debunks some existing ideas about how best to manage high-tech workers and offers new challenges and relevant advice for managing these specialized workers. For academic researchers concerned about the growth of high-tech industries, R&D consortia, and the management of high-tech workers, it discusses recent trends and important research findings in this area.

In the decades ahead, it is expected that high-technology and professional employees will play a critical role in helping the United States regain competitive advantage in the high-tech markets. Most firms can ill afford to alienate these workers, yet that is precisely what is happening in many industries today. Drawing on a decade of research on high-technology and professional employees, this book sets the stage for diagnosing, assessing, and researching the effectiveness of the strategies and practices of high-tech firms.

There are four major thrusts to this book. It begins by discussing the growth of high-tech employees in the work force and the myriad of changing trends facing high-tech firms in the years ahead. The second section identifies the key human-resource concerns of the nineties: how to attract, motivate, and retain these valued workers. This section examines aspects of organizational human-resource systems, with the goal of matching the unique characteristics of the professional and high-tech worker with the demands of their jobs.

The third section discusses the relationship between a firm's culture and the reward systems it employs to attract, motivate, and retain high-tech specialists. Significant attention is given to the role that the reward system plays, principally because much of our existing knowledge is at tremendous variance with current empirical research on how best to reward high-tech and professional workers. An organizational reward systems analysis is offered to help narrow the gap between what the traditional literature has advocated and what the new breed of worker demands.

The fourth section highlights strategies and systems for organizational success, ranging from the design of performance appraisal systems to what structural accommodations can be made for high-tech workers. Career-relevant professional development is also discussed. This section covers not only the management of change but the effects of growing international competition, which has spawned new high-tech consortia designed to simultaneously foster innovation and fend off international threats. A final chapter synthesizes the learnings in terms of success criteria.

Each chapter has both a theoretical and a practical component; current findings support each claim. The relevance of a book such as this should be apparent. There are fundamental and critical differences between high-tech professionals and their organizational counterparts, which demand different types of organizational accommodations. Because high tech has been labeled the "growth engine of the future," we must be able to diagnose and correct unique problems attributable to the aspects of high tech—a label which has subsequently spawned a jargon and a style all its own.

I wish to acknowledge the roles that a number of people have played in the framing of this manuscript. To begin, the Alternative Reward Systems (ARS) group at the University of Southern California has been powerfully influential, particularly on reward systems for high-tech workers. To Steve Kerr, Barry Leskin, Erik Jansen, and Nirmal Sethia—I have cited your work in particular as influential in my thinking. Dannie Mann is also owed a debt of gratitude for her tireless efforts at the computer in typing this manuscript. To all of you, thanks for your support and your care.

INTRODUCTION

1 THE GROWTH OF HIGH-TECHNOLOGY AND PROFESSIONAL EMPLOYEES IN THE WORK FORCE

There is a mystique around high-technology and professional employees in the United States and abroad nowadays. Certainly more has been written about them in the popular media than has been written about any other economic sector. The meteoric growth of high-technology industries since the early 1970s attests to the fact that these industries and the professionals who work within them will be with us for quite some time to come. Indeed, the role of the high-tech firm, and of the high-tech and professional employee, has taken on tremendous importance since the U.S. competitive edge deteriorated in high-tech trade performance in the early 1980s. According to the Department of Commerce, the high-tech growth engine has begun gearing up to meet the foreign assaults on U.S. high-tech performance that began in the late 1970s. Some have gone so far as to suggest that the U.S. high-tech sector may be the only great hope for America's future (Belous 1987).

Whatever the future holds, it is increasingly clear that technology is at the root of our new information age. Equally clear is that knowledge workers—those whose currency of trade is their brainpower—and professionals permeate the fabric of our information society. Over twenty years ago, it was argued that the more advanced a society becomes, the more dependent it becomes on professionals and their expertise. All predictions for the future maintain that knowledge will be the currency of trade and, subsequently, the power base for the professional and technical expert (Klegon 1978; Von Glinow 1985). It is against this backdrop—the glamour and allure of the high-tech industries, the highly skilled professionals, and the ebbing U.S. technological position—that this book is cast.

WHAT IS A HIGH-TECHNOLOGY INDUSTRY?

High technology has been likened to pornography (Belous 1987)— even though we cannot adequately define it, we seem to instinctively know what it is. Yet definitional imprecision clouds our image of who these workers are, and of what they do. Generally speaking, any discussion of high-tech industries and occupations presumes a series of commonalities that Kleingartner and Anderson (1987) and Gomez-Mejia and Balkin (1985) highlight:

- The proportion of engineers and scientists is higher than in other industries.

- New products and production methods are based on scientific applications.

- R&D expenditures are higher than in other manufacturing firms.

- Expertise is valued; academicians are useful providers of training and expertise.

- The products are marketed in domestic and foreign markets.

- The product life cycle is short.

- The management tends to be young and relatively inexperienced.

- Numerous innovations are introduced at frequent intervals.

- There is a high mortality rate for these firms, owing to competitive pressures.

- There is a dependence on outside capital.

- There is less formality and fewer layers of bureaucracy; financial risks are shared more often with employees.

From this wide array of characteristics, four criteria are most frequently agreed upon in defining high-technology industries: (1) employment of technology-oriented workers (for example, engineers, life and physical scientists, and related technicians); (2) an industry's percentage of R&D expenditures; (3) how technology-oriented the goods and services are; and (4) the relative level of the technology employed or developed by the industry (Belous 1987; Riche, Hecker, and Burgan 1983; Dorfman 1982).[1]

Thus, if an industry employs technology-oriented workers, exceeds some level of R&D expenditures,[2] and has workers, goods, services, and current or developing technology that are generally perceived as technology-oriented—then it is said to fall within the high-technology sector. Some industries might fall within that category based upon only one of the above four criteria. For example, if an industry's ratio of R&D expenditures to sales was exceedingly high, it would be labeled as a high-tech industry even if its technology-in-use was at the low end.

In focusing on how high-tech the U.S. labor force is, Riche, Hecker, and Burgan (1983) find that, using a broad definition, over 13 percent of the U.S. work force may be categorized as high-tech workers. (See Table 1–1.) Under the more restricted definition, fewer than 3 percent of U.S. workers may be called high-tech. Based on a projection by the Bureau of Labor Statistics of moderate growth, we can project that the growth of high-tech employment will continue at a somewhat faster pace than overall employment rates. Belous (1987) surmises that "despite this slightly faster employment growth rate, only a small minority of new jobs will be in the high tech sector" (p. 27). Riche, Hecker, and Burgan (1983) note that, depending

Table 1–1. Definitions of the Number of U.S. High-Tech Employees.

	U.S. Labor Force (Percentage)		
Definition of High Tech	1959	1982	1995[a]
Very broad[b]	13.1	13.4	14.1
Very narrow[c]	2.7	2.8	2.9

Source: Reprinted by permission of the publisher, from *Human Resource Management in High Technology Firms,* edited by Archie Kleingartner and Carolyn S. Anderson (Lexington, Mass.: Lexington Books, D.C. Heath and Company, Copyright 1987, Regents of the University of California).

a. Estimates are based on a moderate growth projection by the Bureau of Labor Statistics, using an input/output model of the U.S. economy.

b. The "very broad" definition counts an industry as part of the high-tech sector if its relative employment of technology-oriented workers equals 150 percent of the rate of all U.S. industries.

c. The "very narrow" definition counts an industry as part of the high-tech sector if its ratio of R&D expenditures to sales is at least twice the average for all industries.

on the definition employed—if one were to take a broad definition—approximately 17 percent of new jobs created between 1982 and 1995 will be in the high-tech arena. Those figures and a host of other labor market trends will be discussed further in the next chapter.

High-tech members of the work force are clustered primarily in the following industries (which are generally considered high-tech based on the Leontief-Duchin model): [3] chemicals, drugs, electronic computing equipment, semiconductors and related devices, electronic components, aircraft and parts, communications, robotics, and computer-based instruction (Belous 1987).

High-technology workers in these industries constitute approximately 4.6 percent of the domestic work force and will increase to 5.3 percent in 1990. Table 1-2 arrays occupational groupings in the high-tech industry groups, notes the percentage growth rates between 1985 and 1990 of each occupational group, and computes high-tech's share of U.S. employment.

Judging from these figures, it is not surprising that engineering and scientific specialties represent a significant number of high-tech occupations. More surprising may be the inclusion of jobs that we might be more apt to label blue-collar, such as assemblers, tool and die makers, and machinists. These job categories are vital, however, to many high-tech industries, and in general, most high-tech industries include a large proportion of blue-collar jobs. In electronic components, for example, Belous (1987) notes that 61 percent of the work force is blue-collar, and in robotics, almost 38 percent is blue-collar.

Thus, we come to a fundamental paradox in our discussion of high-technology workers: not all of these workers have glamorous titles or occupational specialties, despite the hoopla around this "new breed" of worker and these exciting new industries. There has been quite a lot of discussion on how the new high-tech worker is somehow doing more exciting, cutting-edge, entre- and intrapreneurial work, which is inherently more challenging, interesting, and clean (see, for example, Kleingartner and Anderson [1987]). Even the firms that house these new workers are supposed to be different, with fewer layers of bureaucracy to wade through. High-tech has been touted as the most interesting of all the industries in which to work. Those not lucky enough to be employed in one of the new high-tech firms are portrayed as wistful for the promise of spillover to their more traditional firms. (Such spillovers occur notably when a traditional firm takes over a successful high-technology company.)

Table 1-2. High Tech's Employment Levels, Growth Rates, and Share of U.S. Civilian Employment.

Occupation	Employment in All High-Technology Industries[a]		Growth Between 1985 and 1990 (%)	High Tech's Share of U.S. Employment (%)	
	1985	1990		1985	1990
Total High-Tech Employment	4,741,394	5,842,926	23.2	4.6	5.3
Electrical engineers	139,648	192,616	37.9	35.9	38.3
Industrial engineers	44,646	58,468	31.0	20.7	22.9
Mechanical engineers	37,847	46,770	23.5	16.1	17.5
Other engineers	102,018	115,231	13.0	18.6	19.0
Natural scientists	56,586	67,027	18.5	17.2	18.0
Computer systems analysts	59,522	80,548	35.3	20.4	18.0
Computer programmers	72,345	99,176	37.1	15.0	13.2
Managers and proprietors	383,606	453,845	18.3	3.6	4.1
Sales workers	96,524	113,708	17.8	1.4	1.5
Secretaries	212,309	211,426	-0.4	4.7	5.5
Machinists	59,050	67,552	14.4	11.1	12.4
Tool and die makers	23,106	26,556	14.9	11.7	14.2
Assemblers	342,435	477,937	39.6	23.5	27.2
Welders	43,284	59,068	36.5	5.7	7.4
Protective service	19,268	24,037	24.8	3.1	3.4
Laborers	88,441	117,091	32.4	1.6	2.0
Janitors and sextons	44,358	58,131	31.0	2.8	3.3

Source: Reprinted by permission of the publisher, from Human Resource Management in High Technology Firms, edited by Archie Kleingartner and Carolyn S. Anderson (Lexington, Mass.: Lexington Books, D.C. Heath and Company, Copyright 1987, Regents of the University of California).

a. High-technology industries are defined as industries in which (1) the ratio of R&D expenditures to sales was at least twice the average of all industries, and/or (2) the relative employment of technology-oriented workers was 300 percent of the rate of all U.S. industries (see Riche et al. 1983: 50–53; Dorfman 1982).

These unblemished images, while true in some firms, are inaccurate for the bulk of high-tech workers. Not all of the high-tech workers are the "gold-collar" workers that Kelley (1985) describes. Not all are generously rewarded—unlike the highly skilled scientists and engineers who command outrageous compensation packages. The high-tech industries listed earlier, using traditional economic criteria, are often fraught with dilemmas—ranging from cyclical demand for products and services, instable employment levels, increasing international competition, and obsolescence. The high-tech workers are often part-time employees and increasingly work off-site, either at home or abroad (Metzger and Von Glinow, 1988). The high-tech industries may be characterized by economic instability and instable employment patterns—hence the paradoxical nature of industries referred to as high-tech. In short, many high-tech workers are unmotivated, change jobs more frequently than other kinds of workers, and are unlikely to spend their careers with one organization (Von Glinow 1985). These factors alone argue for different human-resource approaches to managing high-technology workers.

American management has begun to ask itself a series of hard questions about the attraction, motivation, and retention of these workers. For example:

1. How can the professional segment of the high-tech work force be recruited, particularly in tight labor markets?
2. How can a sense of loyalty or commitment be fostered among these professionals?
3. What type of incentive and compensation package is necessary for these professionals?
4. How can productivity be increased, particularly with respect to innovation and development of high-tech products (Kleingartner and Anderson 1987)?

Since enhancing the professional's productivity is the primary goal of the increased attention to human-resource management systems, it is important to clarify which workers are considered high-tech workers and to distinguish between high-tech and professional workers.

In view of the spectrum of occupational categories listed in Table 1-2, it is useful to think of high-tech workers in bimodal terms—looking at those who are highly skilled and specialized versus those who perform routine, repetitive tasks. Both may be considered more or less professional; it is the purpose of this book, however, to discuss the former—the highly skilled, professional worker—although it should be noted that the characteristics of both types of workers are simply a matter of degree. As with the discussion of high-technology industries and occupations, there has been considerable debate in the literature on professional employees about methods of categorizing these workers. To some extent, the terms *high-technology employee* and *professional employee* will be used interchangeably. But there are some differences that would be useful to highlight at this point.

ATTRIBUTES OF THE HIGH-TECHNOLOGY EMPLOYEE

No studies have been done that identify a set of commonalities for high-tech workers. Undoubtedly, the characteristics of high-tech industries influence these employees significantly, since these characteristics redefine the nature of work, human-resource policies, reward strategies, and management styles (Gomez-Mejia and Balkin 1985). Further, these characteristics have job multiplier effects related to sales, distribution, and servicing of their products, as well as in other aspects of worker behavior. The literature on high-tech workers does not distinguish between scientists and engineers, although both are considered in most current discussions of high-technology workers. If we were to look at the characteristics of engineers versus scientists employed in the high-tech sector, we would note differences between the two groups:

> First, it should be noted that most engineers employed in organizations are not highly professional, and engineering samples should not therefore be used indiscriminatly to test hypotheses pertaining to attitudes and characteristics of highly professional individuals. . . . Second, caution must be exercised when considering data obtained from work groups comprised of both scientists and engineers. . . . Data from the different occupational types should definitely be grouped and analyzed separately (Kerr, Von Glinow, and Schriesheim 1977).

Despite this caution, most writers today continue to group scientists, engineers, and others under a generic definition of "professional" in their discussions of high-tech workers. Such a grouping seems to occur because the high-tech sector is perceived as different from other industrial sectors. Therefore, differences between high-tech scientists and engineers are less obvious than differences between, for example, physicians and lawyers. High-tech industry is characterized by interdependence and teamwork, and thus, grouping of individual characteristics frequently occurs. Although not entirely precise, in the absence of valid and reliable data on the attitudes, values, and behaviors of high-tech employees, such grouping appears cautiously warranted.

Probably the most complete surveys of high-tech workers are surveys of R&D workers. If we remember that the ratio of R&D expenditures to sales was an important criterion in defining a high-tech industry, it is not uncommon to look to R&D workers as representative of high-tech industries. Most such surveys have grouped scientists and engineers together, along with technicians, programmers, accountants, writers, and many others. Miller (1986) describes the R&D professional, and those things that attract individuals to the R&D environment, in the following ways:

- They seek intellectual and technical challenges in the work they perform.
- They see the potential to improve the quality of life.
- They strive for technical "breakthrough" and seek recognition and acclaim from collegial, managerial, and other public onlookers.
- They follow the technological cycles of the field; some individuals are attracted to short life cycles, and others are attracted to longer ones.
- They join a firm because they can relate to the management's beliefs and policies.
- They are rewarded with emotional and financial connections to the firm.

Thus, the "R&D professional" that Miller (1986) describes shares some characteristics with high-tech workers; by definition, however, R&D workers are a subset of the highly skilled, professional high-tech workers discussed in this book.

In summary, although no precise typologies derived from rigorous research exist on attributes of the high-technology employee, most researchers and writers agree that professionalism is the single most important characteristic. Kleingartner and Anderson (1987) sum it up nicely:

> The most salient characteristic distinguishing these highly publicized workers and their work in high tech is, in one word, professionalism. . . . Professionalism thus refers to the skill level of engineering, science and technical workers (their education and training), to the type of work they do, and to the ways in which they do it (p. 10).

Given the extreme emphasis on professionalism, let us now turn to a discussion of the attributes of professionals in organizations.

ATTRIBUTES OF THE PROFESSIONAL— INDIVIDUAL

The term *professional* has come to mean many different things; it has been defined and operationalized in a variety of ways (Kerr, Von Glinow, and Schriesheim 1977). The term has been bandied about with increasing regularity in the media, which has most recently focused on professional ethics, rights, and responsibilities. Precise definition is also confounded by the scientific mystique that shrouds the professionalism label.

We know that there are proportionately higher numbers of scientists, engineers, and other technical specialists populating our large organizations today (Von Glinow 1983, 1985; Miller 1986), and that an abundance of these types of workers is an important criterion in defining a high-technology industry. Further, we know that today's rapidly changing environment has increased the demand for highly specialized professional services, spanning a large range of skilled occupational activity. This has been true throughout our recent history. Durkheim (1952) suggested that such specialization allows our economic sectors to go about their business with a minimum of conflict. More to the point, differentiation and specialization attract different individuals, with different skills, expertise, and values. New skill groups emerge and attempt to control markets for their skills (Presthus 1978). This phenomenon, in turn, leads to professionalization of occupations (Von Glinow 1983).

In some sense, the entire work force is changing to reflect increased specialization, differentiation, and knowledge. Few would dispute that knowledge is power; thus, the new breed of professional worker might be called a "knowledge worker." When viewed from an occupational perspective, knowledge workers are not to be found solely in high tech. They exist in a variety of industries, occupations, and settings. That is why, as mentioned earlier, the attribution of professionalism is a matter of degree. Ritzer (1972), Hall (1968), and others remind us that professionalization should be viewed as a continuum, and that firms and individuals may be placed on that continuum depending on how professionalized they actually are—not on how prestigious or glamorous they consider their occupation to be.

One comprehensive review of the literature concluded that the following characteristics are critical to the professional orientation (Kerr, Von Glinow, and Schriesheim 1977). These characteristics are now referred to as a "consensual definition" of professionalism (Raelin 1985a, b; Miller 1986). They include:

- Expertise—normally gained from prolonged specialized training—in a body of abstract knowledge

- Autonomy—a perceived right to make choices that concern both means and ends

- Commitment to the work and the profession—in short, the "calling"

- Identification with the profession and other professionals

- Ethics—a felt obligation to render service without concern for self-interest and without becoming emotionally involved with clients

- Collegial maintenance of standards—a perceived commitment to police the conduct of other professionals

Few researchers or practitioners would argue that all professionals must score high on all the characteristics of the professional orientation. But these six characteristics do seem to be more descriptive of professionals than of other employees (Miller 1986). Some claim that these characteristics result from professional education and socialization (Raelin 1985a; Bailyn 1985). Others suggest that occupational influence guides the professional orientation far more than the individual "attribute" approach (Freidson 1970; Johnson 1972, 1977; Roth 1974; Ritzer 1972). Since this controversy has guided much of the thinking in the occupations literature, it is worthwhile to briefly consider the debate.

Occupational Characteristics of the Professional

The trend toward differentiated knowledge and the new breed of knowledge worker and high-tech employee caused Freidson (1970) to call for a shift from managerial to occupational authority. Some social forecasters have predicted increases in professional activities organized around a colleague group of equals, with ultimate organizational control exercised by the technical group itself (Bell 1976; Gilb 1966). Many sociologists felt that the individual attribute approach was not sufficiently dynamic or process-oriented to explain the role of the professions. Thus, the power approach was born, signaling the importance of occupational differentiation through the use of political and social influence.

This power approach, favored by most sociologists today, maintains that a professional group can exercise power in providing its services and, at the same time, enjoy freedom from external control. This debate between the individual attribute and power approaches has largely become an academic question. Gerpott and Domsch (1985) suggest that "the view of professions as objectively existing organizations exerting direct pressure on firms to ensure the achievement of a profession's goals is rare at best." They further note that this power approach has been

> primarily used by some sociologists not particularly interested in the implications of their perspective for the management of salaried technical professionals. . . . There is little reason to assume that professional bodies function as effective sources of external control of managers and technical professionals in industrial firms. Hence a look at the collective bases of power of professionalism leads to questioning the utility of this concept as a means for guiding managerial practices (p. 211).

In concluding the debate, it should be noted that only a very few authors have thoughtfully argued for the external control of organizations through professional associations of scientists and engineers (Gerpott and Domsch 1985; Connor 1984; Ellis 1969; Von Glinow 1978). I strongly believe that a greater contribution can be made toward the understanding of high-tech, professional, and knowledge workers by integrating the two approaches. Clearly, both individual role orientation and occupational affiliation influence behavior. Moreover, to effectively manage high-technology and professional workers, both approaches should be synthesized. It is time to depart from the either/or analysis that has so influenced the study of the professions.

Regardless of the preferred approach, the label "professional" has been applied to occupations according to diverse and arbitrary criteria. Freidson (1970: 4) remarked that "virtually all self-conscious occupational groups apply it to themselves at one time or another either to flatter themselves or to try to persuade others of their importance." Such groups seem to share a hunger for prestige, which has doubtful merit as a criterion of occupational professionalization.

Nevertheless, the first categorization of occupations was according to some "prestige" factor; researchers arbitrarily included and excluded occupations from the definitional set. This type of classification permitted the individual's occupational affiliation to overshadow any individual differences. The second approach called for an identification of characteristics by which an occupation might be labeled a profession or a nonprofession. More recently, the emphasis shifted to the professionalization continuum, whereby occupations are classified as more or less professionalized according to the extent that they move up and down the continuum (Kerr, Von Glinow, Schriesheim 1977).

It should be noted here that the approach presented in this book is in no way limited to only the study of scientists or engineers, but can and should be applied to members of other occupations that are too casually labeled "high-tech" or "professional."

A SYNTHESIS: HIGH-TECHNOLOGY WORKERS AND PROFESSIONALS

As mentioned earlier, there is controversy over what constitutes a high-technology industry, a high-technology employee, a professional worker, and finally, a profession. It should be clear, however, that many jobs commonly referred to as high-tech overlap broadly with professional occupations. Similarly, professionals have some of the same values, attitudes, and expectations that high-technology workers possess. It should be further noted that the study of high-technology employees and industries is heavily influenced by, but not identical to, the study of individual and occupational professionalism.

Thus, when I refer to high technology, I will be focusing on the professional segment of the high-technology work force. These high-tech and professional workers are first and foremost knowledge workers—highly educated, autonomous, and career-oriented. We can refer to them as more or less professional depending upon their own professional orientations or those of their occupation. Thus, an integrated definition of high-technology and professional workers will include Miller's (1986) synopsis as well as the Kerr, Von Glinow, and Schriesheim (1977) consensual definition of professionalism.

These new high-technology and professional workers engage in knowledge exchange as the currency of trade and pursue intellectual and technical challenges. Typically, they strive for technical breakthrough to improve the quality of work life (QWL). Their organizational allegiances are suspect, but generally, they join a firm because of the challenge of the work and the management practices. They expect to be rewarded accordingly. They also demand autonomy, abide by a set of ethics, expect to live up to professional standards set by collegial or occupational groups, and tend to have more invested in their skills, abilities, and education than they do in the employment contract with their organization. They prefer to identify with other high-tech professional workers who are engaged in similarly important, challenging tasks.

In short, they are a new breed of worker, with strong professional ties. They create new and very different challenges for the employing organization. They have also helped to create a whole new jargon and new company cultures, which are simultaneously an antecedent to traditional manufacturing firms and a result of changing work force trends. The next chapter examines those changing trends more carefully.

NOTES

1. More broadly, an industry is defined as high-tech if its proportion of technology-oriented workers equals 150 percent of the rate for all U.S. industries.

2. In general, if the ratio of R&D expenditures to sales is at least twice the average for all industries, the industry is said to be part of the high-tech sector (Riche, Hecker, and Burgan 1983: 50–53).

3. This model is a dynamic input/output model of the U.S. economy and provides employment, output, and investment time paths over a number of years. It also allows for changing technologies across industries. For additional information on this model, see Leontief and Duchin (1984), Duchin and Szyld (1984), and Belous (1987, 1985).

2 CHANGING TRENDS IN THE WORK FORCE

Behind the portrait of high-technology and professional workers are significant sociological and demographic labor market factors that are affecting employment and management practices of high-tech firms in the late 1980s and beyond. These changes are evolutionary for the most part, not revolutionary. Nevertheless, they are as dramatic as the postwar baby boom, whose impact upon U.S. society, along with that of the subsequent "baby bust" generations, is quite real. This chapter examines some of these fundamental changes.

THE CHANGING LABOR MARKET: THE GROWTH OF TECHNOPOLII

"Technopolii" are high-tech centers that have been springing up in a variety of places during the last several decades (Rogers and Chen 1987). They include the Silicon Valley, Austin, Texas, Route 128 near Boston, Hsin-Chu near Taipei, R.O.C., Tsukuba Science City in Japan, and many others. These technopolii represent significant changes in the labor markets they serve, principally through creating new jobs, income, products, and services (Rogers and Chen 1987). They also are increasing in importance as governments and organizations dependent on them for new ideas and new products seek competitive advantage in world markets. As such, they represent an im-

17

portant source of social change, and labor market analysts are watching them with some concern. Since these technopolii form the heart of our new information age, and a significant portion of our high-tech labor force is engaged in information work (Rogers and Chen 1987), it is likely that they will predominate in the years ahead. Notable demographic and labor trends affecting or reflected in technopolii include the following.

Increased Diversification of Workers. There are more female workers and dual-career wage earners represented in the labor force today. Over 50 percent of women are currently in the work force. Further, older workers are now heavily represented. Demographers have noted that the median age of workers in 1980 was 30; by 2050, the median age is expected to be 42. Thus, the greying of America is well under way. In addition, foreign-born workers are influencing the U.S. labor markets.

Education. The United States simultaneously has more highly educated people and more undereducated people than at any other time in its history. On the one hand, employment in the high-tech sector generally demands specialized education. On the other, there continue to be low-skilled, unspecialized laborers who demand equal employment opportunities. It has recently been estimated (Leskin 1986) that as much as 80 percent of the dollars spent for management education is now spent in the private sector on in-house training and education and on corporate colleges. This does not include university-based educational programs. Most technopolii have strong attachments to a research-based university and rely on such institutions for both technical and research contributions.

The Decline of Union Membership. A number of forces are affecting the decline, the size, and the influence of labor unions. High-tech employees are frequently not unionized, since professional standards dictate performance. The ratio of labor costs as a percentage of overall costs has new meaning for high-tech firms associated with technopolii, which are interested in global competitive advantage. Thus, a significant new trend is the decline of the labor union.

Increasing Use of Technology. Whether in the office or on the shop floor, there is an increased use of new technologies, which have quietly, and sometimes not so quietly, transformed the nature of our work. It may be hard to believe that only ten years ago there were few if any automatic teller machines (ATMs) or supermarket automatic scanning machines. "Just-in-time" referred more to individual behavior than to inventory control, and videocassette recorders (VCRs) were not commonplace in most households. The office place now has been computerized, and office automation (OA) requires secretaries to perform highly specialized functions. In short, technology has been the single most important change in the past decade influencing labor trends.

Pressure for Productivity Due to International Competition. Faced with a large trade deficit and bedraggled "smokestack" industries, some have called upon the high-tech sector to bail America out of its competitive woes. Yet the United States has suffered from a narrowing technological advantage. Thus, while high-tech exports are expected to remain steady for the next several years in the international markets, high-tech productivity must increase dramatically to compensate for declining smokestack productivity. Furthermore, in many high-tech areas, imports could command a growing share of the U.S. market, further exacerbating the situation. Table 2–1 depicts the U.S. import and export profile in various high-technology industries.

Even in innovation, the classic stronghold of the United States, there are signs that we are not keeping pace with Japan or West Germany. American firms' average yearly expenditures on R&D (1.5 percent of gross national product [GNP]) have trailed behind West Germany (2.0 percent of GNP) and Japan (1.9 percent of GNP), with invention and patent rates declining as well (Kanter 1983).

Migration of Jobs to Service and Smaller High-Tech Firms. According to Mills and Morris (1986), approximately 70 percent of the labor force is engaged in service activities; the notion that the U.S. economy is a service economy has become commonplace. As with traditional manufacturing organizations, there is considerable concern about the performance of these service-based organizations and about methods to upgrade their productivity. Service providers may certainly be found in the high-tech sector, as a quick glance at the different occupational groupings of Table 1–2 tells us. In addition, a huge number of women and minorities have opted out of "corporate

Table 2-1. U.S. Exports and Imports in Various High Technology Industries (*In Millions of Constant 1979 Dollars*).

A. Exports and Imports

Industry	Exports		Imports		Percentage Change 1977–90	
	1977	*1990*	*1977*	*1990*	*Exports*	*Imports*
Chemicals	5,737	8,489	3,996	5,625	48.0	40.8
Drugs	2,161	4,337	897	1,263	100.7	40.8
Computers	2,689	7,295	939	2,730	171.3	190.7
Semiconductors	1,339	3,175	1,305	3,530	137.1	170.5
Aircraft	8,055	13,852	989	2,995	72.0	202.8
Robotics	N.A.	48	N.A.	238	N.A.	N.A.
Total high tech	19,981	37,196	8,126	16,381	86.2	100.4

B. High Tech Net Exports[a]

| 1977 | $11,855 |
| 1990 | $20,915 |

C. High Tech's Share of Total U.S. Exports

| 1977 | 12.3% |
| 1990 | 13.9% |

D. High Tech's Share of Total U.S. Imports

| 1977 | 4.4% |
| 1990 | 6.4% |

Source: Reprinted by permission of the publisher, from *Human Resource Management in High Technology Firms,* edited by Archie Kleingartner and Carolyn S. Anderson (Lexington, Mass.: Lexington Books, D.C. Heath and Company, Copyright 1987, Regents of the University of California).
Note: See Table 1–2, note a, for the definition of high technology.
a. Exports minus imports.

America" in favor of small start-up firms of their own. As a trend, there has been a 43 percent increase in the number of new start-up ventures within the past decade.

The major high-tech start-ups have been geographically concentrated in and around the technopolii, which are currently undergoing excess capacity, temporary market saturation, and international competition (Kleingartner and Anderson 1987). There is sufficient merger, acquisition, and takeover activity now to suggest that much of the high-tech industry is characterized by employment instability, with immediate effects on the size and character of organizations. There are more part-time employees, and unemployment rates can be high. Business failures are much more frequent (Freeman, Carroll, and Hannan 1983).

WORK FORCE TRENDS IN THE EIGHTIES

Employment Trends

Pressures for Full Employment. During the late seventies and early eighties, high unemployment, inflation, high interest rates, slow growth, lagging productivity, and job dissatisfaction became quite significant (Jackall and Levine 1984). Masking the gravity of unemployment among certain populations (for example, minorities and women) during the late eighties was this nation's productivity crisis.

Despite the persistent unemployment, the number of challenging jobs has not kept pace with the education of the population. The government and private industry councils enforcing various job placement programs around the country have tried in vain to match the skills of the unemployed with demands for skills in high tech. The skills do not appear to fit (Kleingartner and Anderson 1987; Jackall and Levine 1984).

Changes in Work Force Demographics and Job Opportunities. The postwar baby boom generation—those born between 1946 and 1964—has come of age and now dominates the middle ranks of management by shaping policies and procedures. These "boomers" are having only half as many kids as their parents did. As such, there will be a critical imbalance over the coming years in the number of younger workers for service and entry-level jobs. Few occupations will be unaffected. As the number of college-age people drops 18 percent by 1995, there will be fewer highly educated employees, causing shortfalls of scientists, engineers, and other high-tech and professional employees.

One would expect that as the demand for these employees increases, their income would simultaneously rise, thus attracting greater numbers of people into these professions. This may not be the case, however, in labor-intensive service industries, the area of largest projected job growth. (See Table 2-2.) *Business Week* (1987) points out that positions such as office clerk and cashier require a

Table 2-2. Where the New Jobs Will Be, 1986–2000.

Largest Absolute Growth 1986–2000

Occupation	Number of New Jobs	Percentage Change
Retail sales	1,200,000	33%
Waiter/waitress	752,000	44
Nursing	612,000	44
Janitor	604,000	23
General manager	582,000	24
Cashier	575,000	26
Truck driver	525,000	24
Office clerk	462,000	20
Food counter worker	449,000	30
Nursing aide	433,000	35

Fastest Growth Rates 1986–2000

Occupation	Number of New Jobs	Growth Rate
Paralegal	64,000	104%
Medical assistant	119,000	90
Physical therapist	53,000	87
Physical therapy aide	29,000	82
Data processing and equipment repair	56,000	81
Home health aide	111,000	80
Systems analyst	251,000	76
Medical records technician	30,000	75
Employment interviewer	54,000	71
Computer programmer	335,000	70

Source: Reprinted from August 10, 1987 issue of *Business Week* by special permission, Copyright © 1987 by McGraw-Hill, Inc.

certain amount of math and reading skills, which thus excludes many uneducated workers. But most highly educated people not only will not accept this type of work, but will not need to if the shortfalls of high-tech and professional employees persist.

These baby boomers have had expectations based on this country's unlimited growth potential—expectations created when the United States was the dominant economic force during the 1960s and 1970s (Leskin 1986). This group also expects various economic entitlements, such as pay, promotions, benefits, and security, that differ significantly from those expected by the baby bust generation (now in their twenties).

The shortfall within the expanding service sector may improve opportunities for older and minority workers. Indeed, we have seen that 9 million new jobs have been created since 1980; 84 percent of those went to women, lending new credibility to the "feminization of the work force" observation. The net result of these demographic changes is that virtually all types of employees are clamoring for greater participation and involvement in decisions that affect their work, jobs, and careers. This is particularly true for high-technology and professional employees, for whom "high involvement" has displaced "quality of work life" as the new term for the eighties.

Alternate Forms of Employment.   In addition to pressures for full employment and demographic changes in the work force, the tremendous shortages of engineers, scientists, and technologists may also be attributable to widespread job disaffection linked to worker turnover, absenteeism, sabotage, theft, alcoholism, and other drug abuse. Perhaps as a means of redressing these vexing employment problems, alternate forms of employment, particularly apparent in the technopolii, have emerged. Unique to the United States in the 1980s, these include, but are not limited to, the following:

- Part-timers
- Supplementals
- Retirees
- "Rent-a-worker"
- Off-site workers (at home or abroad)
- Job-sharing/job-pairing
- "Sunlighting" employees (linked to multiple employers through the computer)

These alternate forms of employment are frequently used to accommodate the special needs of high-technology and professional workers. It should also be remembered that the United States is approaching zero population growth; Mandt (1978) observed that by the late eighties, many firms would perhaps have to scramble to simply attract and retain the number of knowledge workers they need. Thus, these innovative employment structures have been designed to help remedy the imbalance between supply and demand for high-technology knowledge workers.

Alternate Forms of Compensation

There are at least two trends impacting pay practices for high-tech and professional workers that merit attention. I will discuss reward systems for high-technology workers in greater detail in Chapter 5, but will mention here the most commonly cited trends:

Wealth-Building and Wealth-Sharing Plans. The concept of wealth-building and wealth-sharing involves providing a greater return to high-tech employees from an organization's profits than in the past (Leskin 1986). This may take the form of increases in stock options, profit-sharing, gain-sharing and other means of "sharing the wealth" with these valued workers. These plans have in common a short-term incentive plan, designed to reward the employee over a period of twelve months or less, and a long-term incentive plan, which grants awards based on performance over a period of time longer than twelve months. Most short-term incentive plans utilized by high-tech companies involve a pool of incentive dollars distributed on the basis of some measure of performance. Except for the privately held high-technology companies, almost all use stock options as the principal form of long-term incentive (Schuster 1984). The nonqualified stock option (NQSO) is now the most popular vehicle for long-term plans, with the incentive stock option (ISO) remaining popular.

Implementing Pay-for-Performance Systems. The second major trend affecting compensation in high-tech firms is the implementation of "pay-for-performance" systems. These are attempts to better define, measure (evaluate), and subsequently reward performance. Given that most high-tech firms must be able to respond quickly to the rapid growth of technology, it is critical that these firms maintain and increase profitability by constantly focusing on increasing performance. A common theme (expanded upon in Chapter 5) is that, if a firm wants greater performance from its employees, it should be able to reward that performance. Pay-for-performance is one aspect of this equation.

The net result of these two trends—wealth-building and wealth-sharing, and pay-for-performance—is that management compensation has been aggressively pursuing ways to motivate employees to perform, thereby increasing the high-tech business (Schuster 1984). All leaders who have emphasized pay-for-performance in their high-tech firms are increasingly concerned about how to best improve corporate performance, how to use financial and nonfinancial rewards better, and how to escape the "me-too" approach (Schuster 1984) to compensating employees.

Changing Social Trends

As rapidly as technologies are changing in the 1980s, a series of social changes are emerging that coincide with technological growth. As professionals and high-technology workers become an ever more important part of our society, their hopes, fears, and expectations shape organizational cultures. Modern employees are not only better trained and educated, but they have increased expectations about what organizational life will bring them by way of satisfactions and rewards. Since entry into most organizations occurs at a relatively high level for these high-technology and professional workers, they have often been able to bypass traditional promotional paths in favor of the "fast track." When their progress appears to them to be too slow, these workers have been more inclined to quit than their "organization man" counterpart.

Exacerbating this trend is the fact that most high-technology and professional workers have a far greater stake in their own career growth and skills than they do in the success of the organization that employs them. The concept of loyalty to one's firm has been replaced by loyalty to oneself and to one's profession. Of course, American firms encourage this attitude by cutting staff, emphasizing the short-term bottom line, and rearranging structures, teams, business units, and assets through mergers, acquisitions, and divestitures.

Cyclical hiring in some high-tech firms can result in large-scale hirings of employees to fulfill government contracts—as in the aerospace industry—followed by large reductions in work force when the project is completed.

Another social change is the greater emphasis upon psychological and social entitlements within organizations. Human-resource (HR) professionals have forecast the end of the age of economic entitlements, citing a slow growth economy, international competition, and cost-control procedures. Social and psychological entitlements, however, are becoming more important. As already mentioned, modern workers expect to have more say in decisions that affect their day-to-day lives and seek greater personal satisfactions in the workplace. High-involvement entitlements are thus being emphasized more often than pay and benefits, although these traditional entitlements are still being demanded.

Still another social trend, which manifests itself in fascinating ways, is the increased value of entrepreneurialism. The Labor Department has reported that there have been almost twice as many new start-up ventures during the past decade. The organizational analog has been increased intrapreneurial activities, which mirror entrepreneurial ventures.

Finally, there is a new awareness among many high-technology and professional workers of an organization's social and ethical responsibilities. It is no longer acceptable to be cavalier about health and safety within the workplace, and there is increasing attention to smoking, carcinogenic substances, and drug-related issues. Further, there is increased attention to doing the "right" things," whether employment-related or societally-related.

CHALLENGES FACING HIGH-TECH FIRMS
AND THE HR FUNCTION

The magnitude, direction, and impact of these changes have led some observers to note that U.S. society is undergoing a major evolution, similar to the shift 200 years ago from an agricultural to an industrial economy. Whole new industries have emerged that demand talented, educated, self-motivated workers.

In turn, the concentrations of high-tech workers in technopolii are responsible for the development of distinctive human-resource practices, which are designed to attract, motivate, and retain high-technology and professional workers. These practices include alternative reward systems, flexible compensation practices, a move to the corporate classroom for training programs, greater needs in understanding computers, and tying productivity to a firm's business strategy. Maximizing a professional's productivity has led to the adoption or development of new methods of work organization that limit hierarchical levels of supervision, link pay and other rewards to performance, ease the tensions between the competing cultures of professionals and other employees, and give professionals greater participation in the decisions that affect their lives. As discussed in Chapter 7, these concerns have shaped a variety of cultures.

In summary, these distinctive HR practices stem from the managerial needs mentioned earlier: namely, how can professionals be attracted, motivated, and retained in the face of tight labor markets? How can these valued employees be made to feel a sense of loyalty and commitment to a firm? Finally, how can their productivity be increased?

The most frequently cited reason for the failure of high-tech firms is poor management performance (Morrison 1987). These managerial challenges and their solutions are crucial to the success and long-term survival of every high-tech firm. The changes identified in this chapter require different and sometimes counterintuitive management skills and practices. The problems in managing valued human resources will be discussed next.

II ATTRACTION, MOTIVATION, AND RETENTION

3 KEY DILEMMAS IN MANAGING HIGH-TECHNOLOGY AND PROFESSIONAL EMPLOYEES

How can high-technology and professional employees be attracted to and retained by firms in view of tight labor markets? How can high-technology and professional workers be made to feel loyalty and commitment to the firm that employs them? Finally, how can their productivity be increased?

There is very little in our common experience or in the management literature that helps us meet these challenges, since the United States has never really faced the problem of employee productivity (Mandt 1978). It is this problem of productivity, however, that has now caught management's attention; it has been argued that white-collar workers are probably no more than 60 percent productive (Mandt 1978). Since productivity is the demand that sets in motion the need to attract, motivate, and retain high-technology and professional employees, we now turn our attention to the tensions that arise between managers and these workers and that pose key dilemmas for managing worker productivity.

SETTING THE STAGE FOR CONFLICT

The creative and innovative roles played by high-tech workers and the roles played by managers in attempting to control the output and energies of these human resources must be skillfully integrated. In traditional manufacturing firms, productivity is evaluated in terms of tangible output. Much of the work done by high-technology and professional employees, however, is intangible, particularly at the pre-product stage. The production and development of ideas is, at best, difficult to define, measure, evaluate, or control. Furthermore, the success of those ideas may not be immediately visible, particularly when spillover from a good idea may primarily serve to enhance the success of other innovations.

Hence, a fundamental dilemma arises: *the nature of the work performed by high-technology and professional workers predisposes them to resist organizational control.* Highly specialized employees are typically not amenable to conventional bureaucratic control systems, which emphasize a management culture concerned with company loyalty, financial soundness, hierarchical authority and control, and growth in production output, volume, and size (Hower and Orth 1963; Von Glinow 1983; Raelin 1985a). Instead, these workers have frequently attempted to redefine the conditions of organizational participation. There has been considerable discussion on the inevitability of conflict between professional workers and their employing organizations.

Although a certain amount of conflict with clients is characteristic of free agents contracting to perform services, the salaried professional and high-tech worker is additionally confronted with threats to his or her autonomy. That is, once hired, the professional implicitly agrees to an exchange of autonomy for organizational resources (Ritzer 1972; Von Glinow 1983). The professional's reaction to the use of authority for control purposes is probably the most critical variable in the organization's ability to accommodate that employee. This speculation reflects a widely held position that the professional and the bureaucracy are at terrible odds with one another, and that conflict not only arises but is endemic to basic differences between the two, most notably over the legitimacy of each party's authority and control (Presthus 1978).

The organizational position demands compliance from all employees with rules and procedures; the professional's position stems from superior expertise that requires individual autonomy in decision-making and task-related activities. This conflict produces distinctive climates where members are "expected to be loyal to the organization, to behave consistently and rationally according to technical and professional criteria, and to defer to the authority of the organization's leaders" (Presthus 1978: 4).

TENSION POINTS

Specific professional-organizational conflicts may relate to any of the six professional characteristics mentioned in Chapter 1. Each characteristic will be discussed separately, since each one is a salient feature of professional life and resists managerial control (Raelin 1985a).

Expertise

Organizations may find that a professional or high-technology employee's expertise, acquired through specialized training in a body of abstract knowledge, may be too abstract and overly specialized. Overspecialized professionals are labeled "esoteric" and "prima donna." At the same time, the professional can easily become impatient with what he or she perceives as unscientific, or "seat-of-the-pants," problem-solving and decisionmaking by the overly pragmatic organization.

This question of the overly specialized technical professional is not academic. In general, there is a tendency to organizational segmentation in large, bureaucratic firms. This also produces professional overspecialization, by encouraging the individual to become skilled in a fairly narrow area (Raelin 1985a). Raelin (1985) suggests that as long as there is a demand for the microspecialty, there are no adverse effects. But the market mechanism, which efficiently dictates supply and demand, responds quickly to new technologies and advanced knowledge. With increasingly frequent changes, some specialty areas will survive and prosper, but others will become redundant and obsolete. Those employees in the latter category place even more emphasis on what they do know, hoping to overcome their obsolescence and reestablish their importance. Thus, according to Raelin (1985a), each skill group begins to think of itself as superior to and independent of all others.

Further, technical professionals frequently set up artificial barriers between their specialty and laypersons. When the laypersons are the hierarchical superiors, managerial coordination of these different skill groups can become a nightmare. These technical professionals have been known to attempt to isolate themselves from those outside their specialty who are engaged in commercial transactions. One principal managerial task is to coordinate diverse functions of the firm. Raelin (1985a) and others (Von Glinow 1983, 1985; Bailyn, 1985) have noted that the more professionals are able to relax their insistence on highly specialized procedures, the easier it will be for management to coordinate unit productivity. Clearly, the more specialized the various technical functions become, the more they pose specific coordination problems for the firm.

Autonomy

The issue of autonomy has frequently been labeled the most critical problem in managing professionals and high-technology employees (Bailyn 1985; Raelin 1985a). Professionals typically want to make their own decisions about both strategic and operational autonomy. Bailyn (1985) differentiates between strategic autonomy—the freedom to set one's own research agenda—and operational autonomy—the freedom to attack a problem, once it has been set by the organization, in ways determined by oneself. In essence, autonomy refers to having control over means as well as ends. Professionals have argued that they should have both types of autonomy. This right of autonomy clashes, however, with management's expectation about the proper role of the employee. It is unlikely that this managerial expectation will be sympathetic to the professional's desire for autonomy (Raelin 1985a).

High-technology and professional employees generally believe that their work can be performed without constant interference from hierarchical supervisors challenging their autonomy. For the most part, they believe that managers lack the skills necessary to exert any meaningful guidance; thus, they look to others within their technical specialty for help. This dilemma has been discussed and researched for over 45 years now, and it still remains a ticklish problem. Raelin (1985a) and Bailyn (1985) note that most good managers do not take issue with a professional's request for operational autonomy. Many professionals also understand management's need to establish organizational or subunit goals and to specify the methods that will be used to accomplish those goals. It is after the goals have been set, however, when some managers persist in overcontrolling the means of professional practice. This is tight hierarchical control, and it directly conflicts with "expert control."

It stands to reason that professionals will differ in how much strategic autonomy they require. Generally speaking, engineers, technologists, and those who work in "applications" appear to require less strategic autonomy over ends than do scientists.

Collegial Maintenance of Standards

Thus far, it is fair to state that professionals expect to control their own activities with no constraints or interferences from others. They have a concomitant desire for peer control and collegial maintenance of evaluation standards. Most technical professionals feel strongly that they alone are capable of judging the work within their specialty.

We have seen that, as specialty areas emerge and demand attention, management must coordinate these groups and regulate their activities. There is perhaps no greater strain between managers and technical professionals than that produced by this necessity: the use of bureaucratic versus professional standards (Raelin 1985a). Scott (1966) reminds us that managers can rarely achieve the standards upheld by the professional group, owing, in part, to their training, but also to organizational pressures on them to produce. When there is overt conflict over standards, technical professionals typically appeal to colleagues outside the employing organization.

Since the norms of science prevail within the profession, another fundamental dilemma emerges: To whom does new knowledge, created by professionals under the control of the organization, belong? Professionals usually wish to publish the results of their research in scholarly outlets, where peer controls maintain the standard of excellence. Organizations, however, tend to be reluctant to release this information if it compromises their competitive position. Thus, the dissemination of professional knowledge tends to be a point of contention between the professional seeking collegial control of standards and the organization exerting bureaucratic control.

As Raelin (1985a) and others have pointed out, however, many professionals cannot agree on the criteria for evaluating their performance. Some "cosmopolitans" want recognition through collegial maintenance of standards, whereas "locals" tend to be more interested in achieving rank and status within their employing organizations (Gouldner 1957). In general, the applied specialty areas tend to favor organizational evaluation and will more easily forego evaluations by other professionals. Engineers and technologists usually prefer organizational evaluations, whereas scientists generally prefer collegial evaluation and control. It is likely that professional standards will be acceptable to management to the extent that they overlap with bureaucratic standards.

Nevertheless, given the type of work professionals and some high-technology employees do, they will more commonly prefer collegial evaluation systems, and some degree of conflict with management's standards will be inevitable.

Ethics

A professional's code of ethics and orientation toward clients may conflict sharply with an organization's deceptive—either real or perceived—marketing of products and services. The firm's claim of ownership rights and its desire to keep new products and processes secret conflict directly with the professional's desire to disseminate information in scholarly, scientific arenas. Further, when the firm overtly disregards ethical considerations in the use of research results, the professional is tremendously concerned. But from management's point of view, this problem arises because the ethics of the profession are clashing with the interests of the firm (Benveniste 1987).

Codes of ethics define the general do's and don't's of professional service. But they are not always that useful in resolving conflict between organizational mandates and the responsibilities perceived by the professional. This lack of resolution, according to Benveniste (1987), is particularly distressing in our age of increasing technological complexity, when decisions made in single organizations can have tremendous repercussions for the general public and/or for others with a stake in the organization. Problems of pollution and of chemical and nuclear dumps, for instance, have sharpened professional concerns beyond the organizations involved. The crises at Union Carbide and at Johnson & Johnson's Tylenol division have had ethical consequences for vast numbers of people outside those firms.

Key questions have begun to emerge around professional responsibility and ethics. Are professionals in exclusive service to their firms, or are they responsible to the public? Do professionals place the values of the firm above those of the client or the general public? Further, if professionals are acting merely as employees, what does that do to the legitimacy of their profession?

Benveniste (1987) summarizes the concern succinctly: "Professionals in public and private service must be able to convince the general public that they are able to render difficult moral judgments and that they are not using their professional prestige to favor narrow interests" (p. 42). That does not mean that it is easy to upgrade the morality of professionals; it does suggest, however, that management cannot remain indifferent to professional ethics. It further suggests that management needs to be prepared for situations in which professional dissent challenges managerial authority (Benveniste 1987).

Commitment to Calling

The very nature of the socialization process within many of the professions instills a sense of commitment, a love of the work, that has very little to do with the rewards attached to the profession. The very fact that some professionals are supposed to "do good" for individuals and society presumably differentiates these vocations from other work. Benveniste (1987) calls this an almost quasireligious commitment to one's calling, this impression having much to do with making some of the professions far more attractive than they might otherwise be. For example, teachers and nurses are rarely drawn to their professions by lucrative salaries or working conditions. When queried, they usually say that they were committed to the teaching or nursing profession. Some professions attempt to institutionalize this commitment by doing good deeds for the community at large; lawyers are expected to do some amount of pro bono work, for example.

This notion of commitment to one's field affects how professionals and high-technology workers integrate with large bureaucratic firms, because it affects their work motivation. Absent strong extrinsic rewards, strong intrinsic rewards stemming from one's commitment to a professional calling matter even more (Benveniste 1987). Intrinsic rewards are even more important when working conditions are difficult or career and professional rewards are minimal. Much of the mismanagement of these professionals comes from the organization's erosion of their sense of commitment.

External Identification with the Profession

The way professionals identify with their peers, not with their organization, has been the focus of much discussion and debate. Hall (1968) was the first to focus our attention on the belief that the peer group helps professionals keep in touch with advancements in their fields. Since professionals identify to varying degrees with both their organizations and their professions, organizational loyalty is not enhanced when managers downgrade the values of the profession.

All professions define their acceptable practices (Benveniste 1987). Sometimes the universities and school systems lead the professions; at other times, the professions move the school systems ahead. While some professions tightly control who can practice, others do not. Those professions in which client protection is less important generally make little attempt to control member practices. For example, the practice of art does not require state certification, despite the years of training and education that may have gone into the education of the art professional.

Market-controlled professions, however, can be highly competitive. Here, the manager's task is to create productive team experiences that benefit both the professional and the organization, without downgrading professional identity. Given that many professionals are oriented less to narrow organizational perspectives and more to the "greater good" of the public, most managers have some difficulty with this issue. Benveniste (1987) notes that "organizational values and realities are tangible, whereas the "public good" or "doing the right thing" are not easily defined" (p. 49).

Raelin (1985a) further notes that professionals can afford to push for their own standards within bureaucratic structures because of the support they get from the professional associations. The professional associations can exert tremendous social and political influence through disseminating knowledge, updating members on current trends, bringing professionals together through meetings where papers are presented, and accrediting and establishing standards of ethics, conduct, and training. The professional who identifies with the profession over the employing organization can receive considerable support from his or her peers.

Table 3-1. Critical Tension Points Between Professionals and Organizations.

Organizations		Professionals
Hierarchical/ organizational control	vs.	Expert evaluation and control
Rules of the company	vs.	Professional standards
Organizational secrecy	vs.	Dissemination of information
Organizational loyalty	vs.	Commitment to the field or profession
Organizational decisionmaking	vs.	Professional demands for strategic and operational autonomy
Isolate professionals	vs.	Integrate professionals

It has been argued that the tensions between professionals and organizations are so significant that professionals should be isolated from other employees, that there should be little attempt to integrate them into the firm, or that attempts at enhancing their company loyalty would be futile because their commitment will always be suspect. "Dual ladders," for instance, have been created and employed, with marginal success, in an effort to separate the professional and technical personnel from the remainder of the organization. These and other structural accommodations will be addressed later in this book.

Table 3-1 summarizes some of the common tension points between the professional and the organization.

OVERCOMING TENSIONS

Improving the interface between the organizational manager and the professional is not enhanced when the manager downgrades the values of professional and high-technology workers. Those values influence all aspects of their behavior, including their loyalty, their commitment, and their concern for productivity—all of which are equally important to the employing organization.

But as we have seen, managers have some fundamental problems with the values of professionals, and these problems, if unresolved, become knawing dilemmas that lead to questions such as, When should management recognize the concerns of professionals? If in meeting the concerns of professionals, there are potentially damaging trade-offs to the organization, how can these concerns be addressed without provoking alienation and dissent?

This last question is not insurmountable. Benveniste (1987) reminds us that the key question is not whether alienation is inevitable and professional dissent must be tolerated. Management should recognize that a certain amount of dissent is natural, and that the manager's goal should be to understand the nature of this dissent and to utilize it in mutually beneficial ways. "Professional values need not hamper organizational objectives" (Benveniste 1987: 49). Thus, a solution to overcoming the tensions exists in situational analysis: managers need to learn when and where professional values must take precedence over organizational rules and regulations. Similarly, knowing when those values must take a back seat to the organizational controls is equally critical to effective management of the tensions.

In either case, the consequences must be considered because productivity, loyalty, and commitment are at stake. It is unlikely that the firm will enhance productivity, loyalty, and commitment by systematically rejecting the values of the professionals. The skillful management of professionals requires knowledge of and attention to their dual loyalties and allegiances. Failure to do so will inevitably result in mismanagement of these valued resources and in continuing tensions that compete for valuable time.

With respect to the tensions surrounding the professional's desire for strategic and operational autonomy versus the organization's decisionmaking and authority system, the relevant questions that managers should ask are parameter questions. Under what specified conditions should professionals be granted operational autonomy? Under what conditions should they be given strategic autonomy? The resolution of these two questions is not a zero-sum game. Simply because the professional has been granted a certain amount of autonomy over means and ends does not mean that control is taken away from management. That is a common perception, however, in many organizations—that the granting of autonomy to professionals implies rescinding management's control. Sharing responsibility demands cooperation between the managers and the professionals. Both sides can benefit if tasks are accomplished in a more productive fashion. The key is in knowing when to give or take back responsibility and autonomy—the "content" rewards discussed in Chapter 5. The task demands, in addition to his or her skills and abilities, should determine the amount of the professional's autonomy. Making this judgment requires the manager to "broaden the lens" and to wear an organizational "hat," not simply a line or staff hat.

Examples here might include the accountant or scientist involved in basic research in the R&D lab. Neither technical specialist needs to interface with the "outside world." The firm could grant each of these professionals a certain amount of operational autonomy and could differentiate between the two on strategic autonomy. Granting an accountant strategic autonomy would be a mistake, since accountants ultimately calibrate their activities around the goals already set by the firm. The scientist engaged in original and innovative work, however, needs a certain amount of autonomy over the setting of goals and in picking projects on which to expend effort. Failure to grant autonomy to the scientist would probably result in further tension.

The tension of professional standards versus the standards or rules of the firm centers around the questions of who evaluates the professional, using what criteria. This is an inherently difficult and messy issue, since organizational evaluators are often not skilled in the technical specialty they are evaluating, and the criteria they employ may be questionable. The issue of performance appraisal for technical professionals will be addressed at length in Chapter 11; however, the potential for mismanagement in this area is large, so some discussion is warranted at this point.

First and foremost, "productivity" may be difficult to define. There may be numerous aspects of a professional's performance that should be evaluated; but if these aspects are not measured properly, they will be difficult to evaluate. Some of those aspects will be subjective, and others will be objective; hence, the manager must be able to discern which are the most relevant. Objective measurements have the most appeal, since theoretically, performance is grounded in objective, quantifiable output. But a considerable part of the creative, innovative role that a professional plays is highly subjective. Both objective and subjective measurements are filled with difficulties.

When the evaluation of the professional is linked to the reward system, additional tensions accrue. Suffice it to say at this point that conventional methods of performance appraisal are counterintuitive when it comes to managing the performance of the professional. This is why professionals generally prefer to be evaluated by the standards of their field, not by the organizational criteria perceived as arbitrary.

With respect to the tension between organizational loyalty and commitment to calling, it has already been pointed out that it is not feasible to manage professionals by downgrading their commitment to their profession. The calling that they respond to is real and rewarding in and of itself. Benveniste (1987) makes an analogy between the professional worker and the volunteer and suggests that you do not manage a volunteer organization by "constant punishing, making volunteers feel unwanted or providing excessive criticism" (p. 55). Good managers do not punish their people for their commitment; instead, they reward commitment and channel it into organizationally productive tasks and efforts. This is no small feat, since the challenge is to build commitment and loyalty without losing sight of organizational goals. How can a manager induce a professional to behave as though the professional's goals were congruent with the organization's goals (Kerr 1975)? Or, perhaps more difficult, how does a manager inspire a professional to behave as though he or she were the owner, charged with doing a decent job of managing diverse tasks and groups of people? These questions require managers to occasionally abandon or change their own goals. Obviously, these would not be goals of profit maximization. But some goals must be established for the professionals as stakeholders whose interests are represented.

When it comes to organizational secrecy versus dissemination of information, again, care should be taken to allow professionals to take out patents in their own names, to publish the results of their research in scholarly and professional outlets, and to discuss research with professional colleagues outside the firm. The extent to which the manager can reduce conflicting demands on a professional's behavior will result in greater accommodation. Some firms have successfully managed this tension by skillfully recognizing the contributions of technical professionals. This, of course, requires the manager to be alert to the information that the professional wishes to disseminate, which can often be controlled through some type of internal clearinghouse function.

Easing tensions is a key managerial dilemma that is not only a messy problem, but one that defies all the traditional methods of problem-solving. Taking risks and making mistakes are not only parts of the problem, but parts of the solution. Management must realize, however, that there are significant differences between professional and nonprofessional workers. The management of professionals requires understanding the professions and their powerful claims on the individual's behavior.

4 ATTRACTING, MOTIVATING, AND RETAINING HIGH-TECHNOLOGY AND PROFESSIONAL EMPLOYEES

Thus far, we have discussed some of the major characteristics of the high-technology and professional worker and some of the fundamental tensions that exist between the professional employee and the employing organization. These tensions do not exist in an abstract vacuum; the high-technology companies discussed in this book must deal with the realities of continual change. Threats to market share, global competition, and lagging economic performance all provide the impetus for changes in management policies in general, and for changes in human-resource policies in particular. Given the dramatic change in the demography of the U.S. labor force and the increasing growth of technopolii that employ large numbers of high-technology and professional workers, U.S. managers are faced with rapid and wrenching discontinuities in their environments. Under these types of conditions, motivating and retaining existing professional talent, as well as attracting new talent, has become one of the most critical problems for managers. This problem is exacerbated by the exceedingly difficult task of integrating organizational needs with employee expectations.

To remain competitive in a constantly changing global environment, U.S. managers have increasingly turned to new HR strategies to solve their problems. This chapter addresses three related management practices—attracting, motivating, and retaining professional talent. These three efforts repeatedly emerge as high-priority issues

45

for those who manage high-tech and professional employees. With others, I have collected a considerable amount of empirical data over a period of ten years on hundreds of engineers, technicians, scientists, and others identified as high-technology and professional employees. Industries that were heavily researched included oil and gas, aerospace, and electronics companies throughout the United States, including some on U.S. naval sites. The purpose of this research was to investigate which strategies and techniques were most likely to bring about the attraction, motivation, and retention of highly skilled professional and high-technology employees. Which performance feedback techniques were most likely to be accepted by professional employees? How does required task- or resource-interdependence among employees influence the degree to which various appraisal, feedback, and reward systems are likely to be effective? Finally, what is the optimal relationship between an organization's strategic planning and reward systems?

Asking these questions brought in highly consistent responses from managers across an extreme variety of industries. Attraction, motivation, and retention of professional employees emerged as central concerns and are therefore highlighted in this book.

ATTRACTING, RECRUITING, AND SELECTING PROFESSIONAL TALENT

Attraction

For a firm to build a talented research team, or a group of talented specialists, it must make itself attractive to potential employees who have the "right stuff," or the talent the firm wishes to recruit. The competition for high-tech workers and professionals is stiff, not only for the existing talent pool but for new graduates as well. Some firms approach certain kinds of engineering students when they are in their first and second years of undergraduate training, with promises of lucrative employment contracts. The dilemma for many of these firms, however, is that some of these quickly changing technical specialties last only six months to three years; thereafter, the new engineer becomes technically obsolete.

In general, product life cycles in high-tech industries are shrinking; if they are to be economically and commercially viable, they often must proceed through design and implementation phases in less than one year (Miljus and Smith 1987). Thus, the coordination of the marketing and engineering function becomes vital (Riggs 1983). A common problem here is that marketing or sales personnel do not talk to engineers; they do not find out what it is possible to invent, within what time period. "The Silicon Valley is littered with start-up companies that promised the moon, then couldn't deliver" (Gibson 1987). A key challenge, according to one executive, is to couple engineering and marketing concerns when deciding which product-market segments to pursue.

The nature of high tech is change. In many cases, the manager's time problem is exacerbated by the project team being intact for less than two years, leaving the manager with the problems of orchestrating new product development, niche decisions, which types of personnel to employ on which teams, and how to monitor and assess project performance. It is no wonder that, given the chance for error, so many new start-up ventures fail. Firms that operate in these types of volatile environments must be able to adapt quickly if they are to effectively participate in their markets. They must make frequent adjustments to people, work relationships, structure, and even their culture. And above all, they must have the right talent.

It should be reiterated that, through the mid-1990s, the great majority of new high-technology and professional jobs, such as computer programmers, systems analysts, technicians, and engineers, will be in non-high-tech industries (Riche, Hecker, and Burgan 1983). Therefore, companies in need of these types of employees (academic research centers, automobile manufacturers, machine tools and equipment, and a score of others) will be undertaking enormous costs associated with retooling their facilities, retraining their employees, and converting to computer-aided design and manufacturing (CAD/CAM) (Miljus and Smith 1987). Meeting the challenge of these high recruitment quotas includes offering rewards that are salient to these workers. But Miller (1986) reminds us that recruitment begins with meaningful communication about the nature and mission of the firm, including information about its unique characteristics, culture, and work opportunities. The rewards that appeal most to high-technology and professional employees will be discussed in more detail in Chapter 5.

The executives and professionals who participated in my research echoed Miller's (1986) statement. Some mentioned that the literature used to attract professionals was very important, even if it came from ads in the newspaper. For example, "being able to work on exciting projects" in a "nice geographical location" was repeatedly cited as attractive to potential employees. In general, the following factors were cited by respondents in my research as being the most critical in attracting high-tech and professional employees: the type of work they would be engaged in; the type of rewards and benefits that the firm had to offer; the geographical location; the image of the company in its industry as "leading," or cutting-edge; the type of project team, including the reputation of the key players new employees would initially be assigned to work with; the career advancement associated with the position; and finally, the challenge. Admittedly, these concerns affect all aspects of attraction, motivation, and retention. It is interesting to note, however, that these were the initial statements made by the majority of respondents in my research.

Recruitment

An important aspect of recruitment must, of course, be the need to establish relationships with local colleges and universities as a source of talent. Many of the employees surveyed over the course of several years indicated that it was important to cultivate a relationship with the schools providing the technical talent, particularly given tight labor markets. The technopolii generally establish relationships with one or several research universities, and the firms in technopolii are the primary beneficiaries of university talent within their geographical areas. Many of the responding firms indicated that they financially supported faculty research and individual students through grants, scholarships, and internships. Xerox, Honeywell, and Fairchild, to name but a few, all routinely supported research institutes that sponsored students and faculty. Some companies actually became corporate sponsors of the research institutes—to benefit from student and faculty input as well as to avail themselves of current publications, research opportunities, and research results.

Many firms attract professional and high-tech talent through the use of networks and through informal contacts. Former students are frequently used to recruit new talented employees. Similarly, some firms participate in "meet-the-firms" nights at local universities and colleges; such events help recruitment efforts by getting the firm's image out where potential talent can see and become attracted to it. This tactic works best at the entry-level and relatively junior-level positions.

For top-end positions, search firms have become the norm. Here the recruitment pitch takes a different tone: senior scientists are frequently told that they will be able to create their own labs, develop their own projects, and staff these with top-flight professionals. The firm must trade on its prominence, its reputation in the field, and its compensation package, which often includes bringing in others to augment the group, lucrative front-end bonuses, and a variety of other incentives.

It should be noted that professionals in different career stages respond to different rewards, and the high-tech firm that wishes to attract a certain type (age, technical specialty, and so forth) should be aware of this. For example, respondents generally stated that Ph.D. scientists and those engaged in basic research—whether in their own laboratories or in research centers or intrapreneurial units—were more interested in the content of the job, or the "work itself." The primary attraction for these professionals tended to be responsibility, challenge, and autonomy—the freedom to pursue their own projects and interests. Engineers claimed that they enjoyed project stability, job security, and work challenges. They also frequently mentioned career opportunities.

Regardless of what particularly appealed to various respondents, among the concerns regularly voiced was honesty (Miller 1986). Miller (1986) discovered that honesty was one of the most important recruitment techniques. This may sound strange, but employees quickly discover that a firm has been less than truthful in describing a new position if organizational realities are not congruent with the recruitment promises. Given normal foibles in perception, high-tech and professional workers are no less susceptible to perceptual distortion than the rest of us. In general, we see what we hope to see. Our expectations, hopes, and fears influence our initial perceptions, and those initial perceptions may meet with rude awakenings if a firm has not been entirely honest in its recruitment policies. Even if a firm has been honest, there is still room for distortion by the employee, who may feel somehow misled. If the new employee was "promised the moon," and then badly let down, that employee may feel hostile and may cite "unmet expectations." When that happens, the problem shifts to remotivating, or perhaps even retaining, that disgruntled employee.

My survey revealed that job content was the most important recruitment tool. The challenge of working on jobs that "represent tomorrow" and "don't repeat yesterday" headed the list. While other incentives are worthwhile, the job challenge remains the most important recruitment tool available. This will be discussed at length in Chapter 5.

Although high-tech employment is offered all over the United States and abroad, the choice of geographical location rated high among my respondents. In the early 1980s, over half of all high-technology jobs were clustered in ten states (Miljus and Smith 1987). California was in the lead, with 20 percent of the jobs, followed by Texas (14 percent), New York (12 percent), Ohio (9 percent), Illinois (9 percent), Michigan (9 percent), Pennsylvania (9 percent), New Jersey (7 percent), Massachusetts (6 percent), and Florida (5 percent).

The technopolii are also centered in these states, except for Boulder and Colorado Springs, Colorado, and Chapel Hill-Durham-Raleigh, North Carolina. In those areas, there is a growing percentage of high-tech start-ups. The geographical appeal of these locations to potential recruits includes the following: a good supply of jobs in the technical specialty in high-tech–growth technopolii; the strong demand for jobs; the ample rewards and compensation packages associated with these locations; and the encouragement to innovation in these positive high-tech–growth climates.

Further, these locations offer ample opportunity for dual-career families. There is growing evidence that professionals increasingly are members of dual-career families, and therefore, opportunities for the spouse become relevant in attracting top-flight professionals. Also, given the priorities of the "sixties kids," or the baby boomers—to whom leisure and other nonwork activities are more important (Raelin 1985b)—geographical location is becoming increasingly important as a recruitment device.

Another important recruiting device is highlighting the group activities or project teams that the potential employee can participate in. Respondents from Fairchild, a Silicon Valley chip manufacturer subsequently taken over by Schlumberger, indicated that the cohesive aspects of the team or group were strikingly important. Respect for one's colleagues and the enjoyment of working side by side with others in the group or in their fabrication unit were very important to Fairchild employees. This was an important source of motivation and retention as well, not simply of recruitment and attraction.

No matter how junior or entry-level the respondent was, most indicated that knowledge of career advancement was critical. Knowing how they "fit in" with the firm and how they contributed to the firm's advancement was important. As with group cohesion issues, career advancement also seemed to be an important way of motivating and retaining high-tech workers. When the importance of career advancement emerged from relatively low-level high-tech workers, this response initially puzzled our research team. Over time, however, and after repeated administrations of the survey questions, it became clearer and clearer that high-tech workers were highly attracted to firms that gave them some firm sense of career guidance and structure.

Finally, the image of the firm is very important in recruiting high-technology and professional employees. From his own experience, Miller (1986) describes how professionals seem to come from the national labor market, whereas technicians and administrative personnel tend to come from the local labor pool. This means that the reputation of the firm, or the impression it creates, must be "bigger than life." The image of Batelle Research Laboratory, or Stanford Research Institute (SRI), or the Rand think tank, fits that description. Reputation is highly instrumental in achieving recruiting goals. Even those organizations engaged in basic R&D that had a poor reputation—for example, Dow Corporation in the early 1970s—can benefit from the image they have created in the marketplace.

Name recognition is highly important in recruiting talented professionals. This is true not only at the firm level but at the individual level as well. Knowing that "names beget names," it can be a potent recruiting tool to drop a few important in-house names to the potential recruit. An accepted principle among scientists is that working with the person who has achieved breakthrough will enhance the probability that you will achieve a breakthrough (Miller 1986). One young scientist noted that she pursued a noted scientist and took classes and seminars—whatever was available to her—so that she could be exposed to this brilliant individual. In the beginning, the person was somewhat intimidating; however, over time, the scientist became less intimidating as the content of the work became more so, and they became colleagues.

Selection

Having attracted good professional talent, the selection process begins with the project manager identifying the firm's needs, engaging in some type of search, screening applicants, and interviewing potential employees. This selection process is different from others in several important ways, one of which is that the technical specialists meet with other technical specialists, not with HR or staff interviewers. Ideally, the in-house technical specialists would direct the candidate to the lab or project that he or she would be assigned to. Thus, selection of interviewers is very important, since they present the initial "face" to the professional candidate. Since many of the technical specialists who will be doing the interviewing "lack the big picture" or do not think in strategic terms, it is important to school them in issues other than project management. Many engineers, for example, do not deal with other projects, people, or strategic issues until they reach senior levels (Gibson 1987).

The selection process must be sure to include the determination of how close the candidate's skills, abilities, and motivations are to the needs of the firm.

THE MOTIVATIONAL PROCESS

Once professionals have been hired, it is important to continue to motivate them throughout their organizational careers. Since professionals have very different motives for joining a firm and respond to very different types of incentives and rewards, this process, again, is almost counterintuitive. To some extent, the issue is not really motivation, since Freud and others have taught us that all of us are motivated to one degree or another, about something or other. The issue is aligning the goals of the professional with those of the firm—or "goal congruence" (Kerr 1975; Kerr and Slocum 1981). How can the manager induce employees to pursue the company's goal and not just their own goals? Ideally, the company's reward system is responsible for fostering goal congruence, and this will be discussed in the next chapter. But most of the literature on employee motivation (from an applied perspective, not simply a theoretical one) emphasizes the reward/incentive aspects of motivating employees to perform. What is particularly different about motivating high-tech and professional employees is that they respond to different types of rewards.

As mentioned earlier, respondents repeatedly emphasized the "work itself" as an important motivator. In addition, career development was judged to be important, particularly since technical obsolescence threatens almost all technical and professional specialties. Miller (1986) rightly points out, however, that professionals respond to continuing education and development not solely out of a need to ward off obsolescence but for personal development reasons as well. Managers of technical professionals have been slower to discover this fact. But many firms have recently discovered this and are funneling large sums of money into in-house educational programs for professionals. It has been estimated that as much as 80 percent of all monies spent for management education is now spent in the private sector (Leskin 1986). The rise of corporate colleges is evidence that many firms are keen on allowing professionals to upgrade their skills and knowledge. Companies such as Intel, Apple, Wang, GM, Rand Corporation, and IBM now grant degrees for higher education earned "in-company"; this trend is increasing.

Achieving parity with the managerial ladder is another important method for motivating professional employees to perform. Some firms have lost talented employees because the only way of rewarding them was to "push them into management" (Gibson 1987). When employees view such transfers as a distraction from their research agendas, or as a demotion, motivation is affected. Some firms have successfully used dual ladders, which allow professionals to stay within their technical specialty while receiving executive pay and perquisites. Control Data and Medtronic have both succeeded in this venture; however, this structural "incentive" to perform has had checkered success elsewhere over the years.

Obviously, motivating employees to perform is an important topic; it will be discussed further.

RETAINING HIGH TECH- AND
PROFESSIONAL WORKERS

Inextricable from attraction and motivation is retention. Given that turnover in the United States is highest for two categories of personnel—the low-level, unskilled workers and the highly skilled, technical and professional workers—retention of the latter was highly relevant and critical for our responding managers.

Most managers who were surveyed indicated that individualized career development opportunities were essential to initially attracting and subsequently retaining professionals. These opportunities ranged from very stylized career training, such as that offered by Rockwell's aerospace division, to simple career guidance opportunities. The high-tech firms that were most able to attract and retain skilled high-tech and professional employees tended to be the ones that continually sought to improve worker knowledge and skills. Generally, that means not locking people into their jobs and careers (Miller 1986) but, more proactively, discovering the conditions under which professionals sour and then changing those conditions. Raelin, Sholl, and Leonard (1985) have emphasized the importance that job design plays in this process. They point out that this is more powerful than employee participation in avoiding professional disenchantment.

Thus, another counterintuitive method for retaining high-tech and professional employees emerges: emphasize the characteristics of the job, rather than employee participation. Participative management was touted for many years as the solution to the problems of attracting, motivating, and retaining personnel. But there appear to be other, more relevant, structural methods of dealing with these issues. Policy support for career management suggests that, once professionals avail themselves of career changes, the organization will provide jobs that fit their new career stages. Such support has been labeled, "career-sensitive integrated human-resource systems" (Von Glinow, Driver, Brousseau, and Prince 1983). In essence, the professional's career concept helps shape his or her career path, thereby linking productivity to important rewards, job design, performance appraisal, and the like. When the high-tech firm's HR practices are career-sensitive, there is a greater likelihood that professional talent will be retained.

In the end, managers generally tend to do a better job of attraction and selection of talented employees than they do of retention—in part owing to the fact that training and development of professional talent is rarely integrated into professionals' career paths. Obsolescence and burnout can be the result.

Retention is also enhanced by concentrating on specific rewards—including career development support—within the context of the firm's culture. According to our data, the culture–reward system interface is an important relationship in attracting, motivating, and retaining professionals. This will be discussed at length in Chapter 7.

5 REWARDING AND COMPENSATING HIGH-TECHNOLOGY AND PROFESSIONAL EMPLOYEES

The creation and dissemination of information regarding appropriate incentives and rewards is considered critical in controlling the performance of people in organizations (Kerr and Slocum 1981; Von Glinow 1983). Review studies have consistently shown, however, that the administration of traditional rewards, such as promotions, pay increases, and status symbols, is considerably less effective in controlling the performance of professional and high-technology employees. Given the pressure on many high-tech firms to increase their competitive edge, the emphasis on enhancing productivity and organizational commitment has escalated. The most well-respected high-tech firms today believe that compensation and reward systems should be designed to communicate and reward performance that is consistent with the firm's performance objectives.

This chapter focuses on the key elements in compensation and reward system analysis of how to improve the productivity and commitment of professional employees. Because compensation is generally described apart from the overall reward system, the following discussion will first concentrate on compensation as it affects performance. Then the focus will shift to the design of organizational reward systems that take the best elements from current compensation plans and integrate them into systematic plans for rewarding and enhancing performance.

CURRENT COMPENSATION PRACTICES

Nearly every high-tech firm has some type of compensation program. Schuster (1984) discovered, however, that nearly all firms he surveyed believe that their current compensation plans are not doing what they were designed to do. The compensation package that firms offer high-tech and professional employees should ideally be consistent with the contributions of those individuals. Since most high-tech firms emphasize interdependence and teamwork, however, such a compensation allocation can not only be frustrating to administer, but can actually reward dysfunctional activity on the part of key players, resulting in lower overall performance.

In general, most high-technology firms' compensation plans are in the form of incentives (Gomez-Mejia and Balkin 1985). Most incentive pay practices are either short-term in nature or long-term; most high-tech firms tend to utilize both. Incentive plans are often based on the net profit of the firm over a twelve-month period. Bearing in mind that the goal of the incentive plan is to move the organization in the direction its leaders want it to go (Schuster 1984), the incentive component of the overall reward system is designed to be a "carrot that motivates high tech professionals to give their best and remain loyal to the company" (Gomez-Mejia and Balkin 1985: 10). The pay incentives are also powerful signals to high-tech and professional workers that outstanding performance may be recognized and rewarded with cash. Although giving very low or "zero" awards can be given, these are not common (Schuster 1984, 1985), except in companies where strong performance values are part of the culture. This suggests that many high-tech firms pay lip service to paying for performance, but that those firms linking pay to productivity recognize the importance of communicating performance priorities and of paying off for achieving those goals.

Schuster (1984) and others remind us that when incentive awards are given on the basis of group performance, care should be taken to include qualitative criteria in measuring performance. This in turn suggests that special attention should be paid to the performance appraisal and evaluation process. The major dilemma voiced by many managers is how to integrate short-term incentive plans with methods used to reward long-term performance.

Short-Term Compensation Plans

A short-term compensation plan makes cash awards available to professionals based on performance during one year or less. Monetary awards are usually made separately from base salary adjustments (Schuster 1984). Many high-tech firms use short-term incentive plans throughout the organization, not only for senior executives or for those four to six levels down from the chief executive officer.

The short-term incentive plan is important for several reasons. Gomez-Mejia and Balkin (1985) note that it is helpful in maintaining an egalitarian culture that rewards technological innovation. The employees who participate in short-term incentive plans are better able to identify with the firm's financial goals, thus sharing a sense of community. Second, short-term incentive plans communicate powerfully those messages the firm wishes to emphasize: for example, growth indices, market share, and the like. Third, they provide management with considerable flexibility in allocating compensation according to the overall company performance. This type of strategy can reduce the fixed-pay component, while maximizing variable rewards by spreading the risk around. Profit-sharing and cash bonuses are the most commonly used short-term pay incentives (Gomez-Mejia and Balkin 1985).

Profit-sharing plans allow all employees to participate. If the firm is large enough to have many different divisions, profit-sharing will most likely be based on each division's performance. In cases where profit-sharing is a function of the firm's overall performance, managers tend to be less satisfied (Schuster 1984), on the grounds that some divisions operate in tough growth markets, whereas others do not. The company generally sets aside a predetermined percentage of pretax profits to share with the employees if the firm achieves its financial targets (Gomez-Mejia and Balkin 1985). If the target has been successfully reached, employees generally receive lump sum awards.

Cash bonuses are somewhat more flexible in that they can be based on attaining financial or nonfinancial group performance goals. The flexibility is important, since it allows for qualitative criteria: for example, achieving technological breakthrough, or completing a project ahead of schedule (Gomez-Mejia and Balkin 1985).

Cash bonuses are frequently made in lump sum amounts and on a one-time basis.

Long-Term Compensation Plans

A long-term compensation plan grants awards based on performance over a period of time longer than one year. It is designed to reward sustained performance that is consistent with the goals of the firm (Schuster 1984). Unfortunately, some of the short-term goals, rewarded by short-term incentive pay, conflict with the firm's long-term goals. For example, concentrating on achieving quarterly targets rather than on new product innovations may lengthen the time it takes to achieve new product profitability. When that happens, the firm is caught in a bad situation; employees continue to get short-term profit-sharing bonuses, but are never motivated by long-term incentives. The firm mortgages its future that way.

Stock options and stock purchase plans are popular long-term incentives. Stock options involve the granting of company stock to initially attract and then to reward managers. In the early stages of a high-tech firm's growth, venture capitalists play a large role in providing leadership and management of the firm. The founder, or entrepreneur, generally has an equity position, and the remainder of common stock will be owned by the venture capitalists. The objective is to increase shareholder wealth; thus, these individuals often participate in the design of long-term incentive plans that involve issuing common stock to attract and reward key players (Schuster 1984). In the early stages of a start-up high-tech venture—when the "liability of newness" is most likely to be fatal—stock options can be given to many members of the company, including secretaries. After the firm goes public, however, it is more likely that stock options will be used less often.

Stock purchase plans are long-term incentive plans for firms trading stock on the public market. Under these types of long-term plans, employees are able to purchase company stock at a discount from market price, generally ranging from 15 to 20 percent (Gomez-Mejia and Balkin 1985). The firm makes up the difference.

Both long-term plans attempt to motivate the employee to think more in terms of the long run. For the innovators—the scientists and engineers who are considerably removed from the commercial aspects of the projects they are working on—these long-term incentives take on a very real importance (Gomez-Mejia and Balkin 1985).

But both short-term and long-term incentive plans have their problems. A large multidivisional firm like Westinghouse, for example, does not have just one incentive formula, since each business unit is very different. In general, high-tech firms tend to focus on specific units as profit centers. In those cases, the compensation is meant to reflect the performance of the unit rather than that of the corporation as a whole (Reibstein 1987). Many firms are beginning to drop the long-term stock option incentives, which are based on corporate results, in favor of long-term divisional targets for some select number of employees (Reibstein 1987). (Honeywell was among the first group of companies that tailored its long-term plans to specific unit performance.)

Table 5-1 shows compensation differences among high-tech firms. Milkovich (1987) notes that no single survey analyzes all pay policy decisions under short-term and long-term incentive systems; the relative competitiveness of the total compensation package; internal equity of hierarchies; and the performance emphasis. For comparative purposes, however, the following analysis focuses on firms with extensive high technology versus those that are more traditional—large bureaucratic firms with limited high technology. In general, high-tech firms tended to emphasize incentives and to extend incentives to people throughout the organization. Traditional firms emphasized base salary more, along with merit increases, and limited the long-term incentives to upper-level employees and a few key technical personnel (Milkovich 1987).

Widespread disaffection with both short-term and long-term plans has caused some firms to look long and hard at what they want their managers to do to obtain financial rewards. Some firms are investigating long-term plans that do not use financial criteria at all (Schuster 1985).

Compensation specialists agree that managers are the ones who are ultimately responsible for making human assets profitable. They also agree that it takes a considerable amount of energy to motivate high-tech and professional employees to "buy into" the corporate culture and to espouse the company's goal. Both short-term and long-term incentive compensation plans are necessary, but not sufficient, for achieving goal congruence. That insufficiency can be explored in a deeper analysis of organizational reward systems.

Table 5-1. Compensation Practices Across Firms for Technical and
Managerial Employees.

Pay Policy Decisions	Degree of High Technology	
	Extensive	Limited (Traditional Firms)
Mix of pay forms	Incentives and base salary emphasized	Base salary and merit pay emphasized
	All technical employees eligible	Limited eligibility by organizational level
	Wide range of "perks" and services available	Wide range of "perks" and services available
Competitive position	Most tend to meet competition; some lead	Most tend to meet competition; some lead
Internal hierarchies	Widespread use of formal job evaluations	Widespread use of formal job evaluations
	Dual career paths for technical employees	Limited use of dual career paths
Performance emphasis	Widespread use of bonuses for all technical employees	Limited use of bonuses for technical employees
	Moderate use of profit-sharing	Limited use of profit-sharing
	Widespread use of stock ownership plans	Limited use of stock ownership plans
	Moderate use of long-term stock options	Limited use of long-term stock options

Source: Reprinted by permission of the publisher, from *Human Resource Management in High Technology Firms*, edited by Archie Kleingartner and Carolyn S. Anderson (Lexington, Mass.: Lexington Books, D.C. Heath and Company, Copyright 1987, Regents of the University of California).

ORGANIZATIONAL REWARD SYSTEMS

The term *reward system* is used to refer to a series of interrelated elements: (1) the type of rewards that are available in a firm; (2) the conditions under which different rewards are made available to individual employees; and (3) the ways in which these rewards and the criteria for their allocation are selected and administered in a firm (Kerr 1975; Sethia and Von Glinow 1985).

Figure 5-1. Reward System Practices.

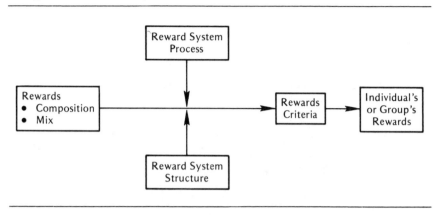

Lawler (1984) argues that reward systems are broader than compensation systems, and that they comprise core values, structures, and processes. *Core values* represent the firm's philosophy in selecting and distributing rewards; *processes* refers to communications and the ways in which people are involved in developing reward practices. Drawing on the work of Kerr (1983) and Lawler (1984), an organization's reward system can be conceptualized as "the various rewards available and their salient characteristics, the criteria according to which members get these rewards, the process of selecting and distributing these rewards and communicating about them, and the administrative structure which governs these rewards" (Sethia and Von Glinow 1985). The relationship of the components of the reward system is shown in Figure 5-1.

The criteria for allocating rewards typically fall into three categories:

- Results of performance: tangible outcomes in individual, group, division, or firm performance; quantity and quality of performance

- Performance actions and behaviors: teamwork, cooperation, risk-taking, creativity

- Nonperformance considerations: customary or contractual; type of job, nature of work, equity, tenure, level in hierarchy, and so forth are rewarded.

Very little research has been done on the structural and procedural aspects of reward system practices, or on the strategic implications of designing reward systems. Jansen (1987) and Kerr (1984) have both sought to illuminate some of the strategic implications of reward systems; however, most research on reward systems focuses on pay policies and on very little else. Even diminishing the focus to pay policies only, the most well-respected consulting groups working on compensation policies do not agree on allocation of incentives. Milkovich (1987) points out that, when comparing the recommendations of Hay Associates with those of Arthur D. Little, one can see some fundamental differences in prescriptions, particularly around rewards. He further points out that "no reliable basis exists for advising which, if either, policy option will pay off in terms of desired employee behaviors and firm performance" (p. 113). This suggests that there may be organizational conditions under which a variety of incentives and rewards will be appropriate. The key is to uncover those conditions.

When these issues are coupled with the special case of professional and high-technology employees—whose values, goals, and expectations differ from those of traditional employees—the strategic design of organizational reward systems is one of the most critical, but least understood, phenomena in the United States today (Von Glinow 1985).

Kerr (1988) has argued that an effective reward system is one that

> takes as given the existence of incongruities in member goals and motives, and seeks to reduce these through intelligent use of quid pro quos. . . . Rather than regarding man's "selfishness" as an insurmountable barrier, an effective reward-punishment system takes the personal goals of people as a fact of life, and uses these personal goals to stimulate participation and performance . . . [because] it is in their personal best interests to do so (p. 5).

Most reward systems, however, are far from perfect. To some insiders, as well as some outsiders, these reward systems may appear to reward behaviors that are antithetical to firm goals and undesired by the rewarder, while virtually ignoring or punishing desired behaviors (Kerr 1975, 1988). Furthermore, these systems may offer technical professionals rewards that are not particularly desired by those employees. Many firms are notorious for offering professionals rewards they do not want and then wondering why these professionals leave or are pirated away for an insignificant pay increase (Von Glinow 1985). It has become increasingly clear that organizations must establish different and separate reward systems for their high-technology and professional employees. Not doing so will ensure the inability to attract, motivate, and retain these valued human resources, through lack of attention to the power of the organizational reward system.

REWARD SYSTEM DIAGNOSTIC

As has been mentioned briefly in Chapter 4, some of the most important sources of motivation, satisfaction, and retention of high-technology and professional employees are the nature of the work itself, the organizational processes, and career development (Miller 1986; Griggs and Manring 1986; Von Glinow 1985). Griggs and Manring (1986), among others, have pointed out that, while these concerns may vary in importance, the most powerful sources of variance were explained by the respondent's age and the company's culture. These will be discussed later. At this point, diagnosis of reward systems as they affect high-technology and professional employees begins with the following key questions.[1]

What Are the Salient Rewards?

A logical first step in diagnosing a firm's reward system is to identify the rewards that are seen as attractive to respondents. Kerr (forthcoming) reminds us that the operative word is *reinforcer*, not *reward*; however, at the beginning of the diagnostic it is difficult to know which rewards will, in fact, be reinforcing. He goes on to describe three generally distinct categories of rewards: (1) financial or economic rewards, (2) prestige or social status rewards, and (3) job content rewards. To that list I have added two categories from my research on reward systems for high-technology and professional employees: (4) career rewards and (5) professional rewards.

Financial or Economic Rewards.   It is widely believed that money and related financial rewards are the best stimulus to employee performance (Lawler 1971). These financial rewards include pay, fringe benefits, bonuses, and so forth.

Prestige or Social Status Rewards. These rewards earn the worker the respect, or envy, of other people in the firm. Status or prestige awards do not necessarily have a financial component. Having a windowed office, having a title, or driving a company car are typical social status rewards.

Job Content Rewards. These rewards have more to do with the "work itself" than with financial or status aspects of the job. These rewards allow individuals to satisfy important needs and goals (Kerr 1988). Doing "important" or "interesting" work, or being challenged, are examples of this category of rewards.

Career Rewards. Having more to do with enhancing personal careers, these rewards highlight growth and longevity prospects. For example, job security, training, development, and opportunities for advancement are all considered career rewards.

Professional Rewards. These rewards have been shown to consistently attract, motivate, and retain high-technology and professional employees. Examples include: having autonomy with respect to means-ends decisions; freedom from tight supervisory controls; ability to pursue continuing education; and peer evaluation and control.

The judicious combination of these categories of rewards to stimulate the productivity and efforts of professional and high-technology workers will be discussed in Chapter 6.

How Are These Rewards Obtained?

Having identified a battery of rewards that are meaningful to respondents, the next step is to determine how they actually receive rewards. In general, organizational rewards are given for one or a combination of the following factors (Kerr 1988):

1. Individual performance: Workers must perceive that the reward for results, actions, and behaviors will be received if they perform well and will not be received if they perform poorly.
2. Group performance: Members of a working unit must perceive that they all share in the distribution of a group reward only if the group performs well.

3. Attendance: Coming to work on time and at least looking results-oriented if not actually being results-oriented are behaviors meriting "attendance" rewards.
4. Membership: Simply signing their names on employment contracts brings workers "membership" rewards. Some types of membership rewards are fixed, that is, all members receive them upon entering the firm. Other membership rewards are variable; for instance, one must be a member for a certain amount of time to receive some membership rewards.
5. Hierarchical level: Having reached a certain level in the firm activates this reward.
6. Other: Sometimes rewards are given for reasons other than those listed above. Politics, for example, can influence the distribution of rewards.

Who Controls the Distribution of the Rewards?

The next step is to determine, based on respondents' perceptions, who or what controls the distribution of rewards. The control of rewards is usually exercised by some combination of the following (Kerr 1988):

1. Organizational policy: The firm has guidelines or regulations affecting the distribution, of rewards.
2. High-level management: The distribution of rewards is determined by someone at a higher level than that of the respondent's immediate superior.
3. The union: In unionized firms, the contract in force specifies which rewards are to be given.
4. Human-resource group: In some firms, the HR function directs the distribution and the timing of rewards.
5. Immediate superior: The respondent's direct superior is the one who controls the distribution of rewards.
6. Self: The respondent personally controls the distribution of rewards.
7. Automatically, over time: The rewards accrue for either fixed or variable membership, automatically.

Which Activities and Behaviors Are Rewarded and Punished?

This section of the diagnostic gathers respondent perceptions of what would happen to them if they were to do certain things or behave in certain ways. Having identified what the important goals of the division, work group, or unit are, the respondents are asked to describe the activities and behaviors that are instrumental in achieving those goals. Respondents are then asked to predict whether they would receive approval or disapproval if they performed those actions, or if they would be unable to make a prediction.

Implications for Rewarding High-Technology and Professional Employees

Having administered the above diagnostic to many organizations, Kerr (1988) has noted that "organizations often do not get the member behaviors their leaders claim to want, but they invariably get the behaviors which these leaders' subordinates believe are rewarded" (p. 19). For high-technology and professional employees, the irony becomes apparent: organizations seek to reward behaviors and actions that contribute to organizational goals, but many firms inadvertently reward behaviors and actions not linked to organizational performance. Given the difficulty in differentiating rewards that are salient for high-tech and professional employees from those appealing to their organization-man counterparts, it is no wonder that so much confusion exists around which pay practices or other incentives are best suited to them. If the firm "pays off" for the wrong types of behaviors and actions, owing to structural deficiencies in the reward system, how then can it expect to reward high-tech employees except by happenstance? Given the earlier assertion that more than one set of incentives may be correct for any strategic situation, the picture is tremendously confounded.

The use of the reward systems diagnostic can help identify which rewards are most salient to high-tech and professional employees and, in addition, can help determine the extent to which those rewards are performance-contingent. Further, the diagnostic can help determine where a gap exists between actions and rewards. Chapter 6 begins to uncover some of the gaps in traditional systems by closely examining rewards for high-technology and professional employees and by offering a series of scenarios about dysfunctional and functional reward systems.

NOTE

1. This reward system diagnostic, described briefly in this chapter, is the result of the work of a group of reward system diagnosticians called Alternative Reward Systems (ARS). The reward systems work was initiated by Steve Kerr, following his seminal 1975 article, "On the Folly of Rewarding A While Hoping for B." The group—composed of Steve Kerr, Barry Leskin, Mary Ann Von Glinow, Erik Jansen, Nirmal Sethia, and Susan Hocevar—participated in a considerable amount of research, initially funded by the Office of Naval Research, on dysfunctional aspects of organizational reward systems in such organizations as AT&T, Honeywell, Arco, Sun Company, Natomas, and others. The diagnostic is more fully described in Kerr (1988).

THE RELATIONSHIP BETWEEN ORGANIZATIONAL CULTURES AND REWARD SYSTEMS

6 MATCHING REWARD SYSTEMS TO HIGH-TECHNOLOGY AND PROFESSIONAL EMPLOYEES

As discussed in Chapter 5, the design of an organization's reward system should be predicated on a series of diagnostic questions: What are the salient rewards? How are these rewards controlled? To what extent are these rewards performance-contingent? To what extent are the professional's actions rewarded or punished?

Answers to these questions begin to better focus the manager's attention on how to satisfactorily attract, motivate, and retain high-tech and professional workers. Having noted with some dismay that scholars and managers agree that there seem to be no consistently reliable *incentives* for producing the desired employee actions, this chapter seeks to map out which *rewards* have had the most success in motivating professionals to perform.

WHAT ARE THE MOST COMMON REWARDS?

It seems that compensation specialists and HR personnel dedicated to attracting, motivating, and retaining high-tech and professional employees are generating increasingly new, complex, and creative compensation packages. High starting salaries for new college graduates, coupled with generous benefit packages, have been cited as essential (Miljus and Smith 1987). Among the many and complex benefits heralded as motivating professionals to perform, the most frequently cited include: relocation allowances, front-end bonuses, front-end paid vacations, settling-in allowances, tuition reimbursement, continuing education reimbursement, assistance with new home purchase and sale, dual ladders, and retirement and health benefits packages. Long-term equity arrangements do not work particularly well with new college graduates; however, short-term and long-term incentives, such as profit-sharing and stock options, are increasingly given to key contributors to the high-tech firm.

Cash still appears to be the most heavily favored vehicle in "key contributor" programs. Key contributor programs are yet another attempt to recognize and reward high-tech and professional workers judged to be the key players. In a 1985 study, Hay Associates determined that 76 percent of the firms in their sample of sixty-four high-tech firms participated in a formal or informal key contributor plan (Spratt and Steele 1985). The rationale among these firms for creating a key contributor program was generally that the reward and compensation systems in use left managers little leverage to focus efforts on critical projects. Further, the existing systems did not enable firms to retain valuable high-tech and professional employees. The newer key contributor plans offered the following creative vehicles to reward key technical and professional contributors (Spratt and Steele 1985):

1. Cash, typically a spot award or lump sum award ranging from $5,000 to $30,000, was used by 88 percent of the responding firms.
2. Equity, in the form of stock options or stock grants, was used by 54 percent of the responding firms.
3. Special benefits or perquisites, such as automobiles, sabbaticals, and trips, were used by 35 percent of the responding firms.

Hay Associates were quick to point out that, although there have been a few effective key contributor programs, in general they do not live up to their initial rave reviews or to their potential for motivating high-tech people to perform. They observed that most key contributor programs are informal, are not well communicated to all potential key contributors, and are far too conservative in their rewards to have significant motivational or retentive value. Perhaps the most damaging criticism of key contributor progams is that too often a single program is expected to work for all key contributors.

Figure 6-1. The Performance-Reward Relationship.

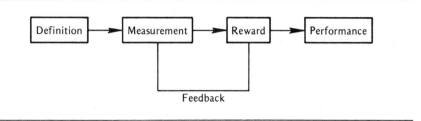

Thus, while some incentives may work for many people, it is naive for system designers to assume that one reward system will work for everyone. People in general, and high-technology and professional workers in particular, respond to different rewards and incentives. Some forward-thinking firms recognize that fact and are attempting to differentially reward workers, not simply through key contributor programs but by matching rewards with individual contributions. Chapter 7 examines the cultural context within which this occurs. At this point, however, it should be noted that if incentives and rewards are to be useful at directing and motivating behavior, they must be attractive to the recipients. Further, for any incentive or reward system to be useful, a manager must believe that he or she has some degree of control over what is being measured. Kerr (1975) identified a model for directing performance, identifying salient rewards, measuring and evaluating performance, and giving feedback. Figure 6-1 portrays this process:

The premise is that performance is the output; if a firm wants performance, it must be able to reward it. In the absence of a strong reward system, it is most likely that performance will be spotty. To reward it, however, a firm must be able to measure performance. If performance measurement is impossible or difficult, chances are that it will be less precisely rewarded. Imprecisely rewarded performance is questionable.

Further, performance measurement is predicated on accurate definitions of performance. What is not defined as performance will be neither measured nor rewarded. Aspects of performance that are not rewarded will most likely not be engaged in by high-tech and professional employees. That, of course, can include even those actions that are most needed for performance to occur. If those actions are not rewarded, it is not likely that performance will occur.

Finally, for rewards to be a useful barometer of performance, employees need to understand that the actions or behaviors for which they were rewarded have indeed been measured. That understanding occurs through the feedback process. To make a reward system diagnosis with respect to high-tech and professional employees, let us begin with the rewards themselves, to see which rewards are most salient to professional and high-tech workers.

What Are the Most Valued Rewards?

Over a period of seven years, data were collected, using instruments designed by the ARS group, to determine which rewards were most valued by organizational members. Responding firms included Sun Company, ARCO, Rockwell, First Interstate Bank, Natomas, and AT&T. High-tech and professional workers constituted more than 50 percent of these companies' workers. Thus, a diagnostic for ascertaining rewards most salient for high-tech and professional workers was developed.

The following are the key rewards most valued by high-tech and professional workers:

A. *Professional Rewards*

1. Opportunity to work with top-flight professionals
2. Freedom to make the most of your own work decisions
3. Intellectually stimulating work environment
4. Not working on repeating yesterday, but working on tomorrow
5. Having an impact on national legislation

B. *Job Content Rewards*

1. A productive atmosphere
2. Flexible work hours
3. Long-term project stability
4. Opportunities to address significant human needs
5. Diversity of business, which creates continuing new opportunities
6. Patriotic projects
7. Projects of an altruistic nature

C. *Career Rewards*

1. Working for a leading-edge company
2. Diverse opportunities for personal growth and advancement
3. Opportunity to participate in the company's successes
4. Career opportunities to stay ahead of the crowd
5. The chance to get in on the ground floor of important projects
6. Opportunities for self-expression
7. Being able to play a role in the company's future

D. *Social Status or Prestige Rewards*

1. Beautiful location
2. Open-door management
3. Extensive recreational facilities

E. *Financial Rewards*

1. Twice-yearly salary reviews
2. Compensation for unused leave
3. Cash bonuses

As illustrated in this list, and as stated elsewhere, the most important rewards are professional and job content rewards. Depending upon the age of the respondents or upon the company culture, these rewards are differentially valued. This is critical for a company to recognize: people change in their values and in their work orientations, depending on career and life stages.

For example, our data reveal that people in their twenties respond to job content rewards and to some financial rewards; people in their thirties respond to professional, career, and job content rewards; people in their forties respond to professional, career, and job content rewards; people in their fifties respond more to social, financial, and career rewards; and people in their sixties respond to financial and social status rewards.

The discussion about company cultures will continue in Chapter 7; however, it is not unreasonable to suggest that a firm's culture and its reward system are intricately intertwined (Sethia and Von Glinow 1985; Von Glinow 1985).

These valued rewards are arrayed in the above list in accordance with how salient they are to high-tech and professional employees.

It is interesting to note that traditional monetary and nonmonetary rewards rank relatively low on the list of rewards valued by these employees. This finding is consistent with that of others who have attempted to discern the relative salience of pay and bonuses, or financial incentives, as compared with other incentives and rewards (Griggs and Manring 1986; Miller 1986; Von Glinow 1985). Generally speaking, financial rewards do not rank in the upper quarter of valued rewards. While they are useful in many respects, they do not contribute to motivation or retention of high-tech and professional workers.

Financial Rewards Lack Leverage in Motivating Professionals to Perform

In general, financial rewards are weak motivators, and still weaker as retention devices. While cash bonuses have some appeal—particularly to those in their thirties and forties—it is important to note that the money itself is significantly less important than any of the other kinds of rewards. This observation dovetails with my earlier contention that professionals feel a commitment to calling; they value the work they do *not* because of the financial incentive, but because of the work itself.

Also notable is the apparent lack of interest in stock options, as compared with cash bonuses, as an incentive to stay with the high-tech firm and contribute to its growth. This finding has also been supported in the empirical literature (Griggs and Manring 1986).

Why then do theorists and others interested in compensating and rewarding high-technology and professional employees insist on concentrating on financial rewards? Perhaps they wish to give employees "a role to play in the company's future," or "an opportunity to participate in the company's successes." Whatever the reason, it is increasingly clear that it cannot be determined which pay options pay off in terms of employee behaviors and firm performance (Milkovich 1987) because pay and other financial rewards are not extremely meaningful to high-tech and professional workers. This finding is counterintuitive to much of the compensation literature, which discusses new and exquisitely complex compensation and pay policies.

It is fascinating to note, from a behavioral perspective, that no single stock incentive was ranked in the upper quarter by any age group in either my research or that of others (Griggs and Manring [1986], for example) interested in determining reward salience. Further, special income awards were not particularly valuable to these workers. In the final analysis, it is the professional, career, and job content rewards that appear to be most valued by professionals and high-tech workers.

MATCHING VALUED REWARDS TO PROFESSIONALS' CHARACTERISTICS

The purpose of a reward system is to give people an incentive for attending and a reward for working. As mentioned in Chapter 5, the different types of rewards may be judiciously combined into a reward system for high-technology employees. The extent to which the various combinations of rewards induce professionals to perform—the "test" of reward systems—is the subject of Chapter 8.

In the meanwhile, it is very important to reiterate the research findings presented in this book and in that of many others: *Overall, the most important sources of attraction, motivation, and retention of high-technology and professional employees derive from the professional rewards associated with the work itself, from the career development process, and from the organizational processes (including how the work is evaluated, how autonomous the workers are, and how well people work with one another). Important sources do not include financial or economic rewards, of either a short-term or long-term nature.*

When these incentives are matched with the characteristics of the professional and high-tech employee, a new schema emerges: incentives matched to the individual values and beliefs of the professional.

Chapter 1 highlighted the characteristics of the professional and high-technology worker, and they are summarized in Table 6–1. Each characteristic will be considered separately in light of the incentives that implicitly match the professional's value orientations.

Expertise

Organizational incentives ideally should provide for the maintenance and growth of the professional's skills over time. The purpose would

Table 6-1. Organizational Incentives for Professionals.

Professional Characteristic	Organizational Incentives
1. Expertise	• Provide for maintenance/growth of professional skills over time to avoid obsolescence • Quality of facilities (space, privacy, equipment) and facilitative support services • Leaves of absence, seminars, management, training, sabbaticals (15-20 percent of base salary) • Development counseling (career-shifting)
2. Ethics	• Reduce conflicting demands from colleagues, superiors, and clients • Allowing information-sharing with referents outside the firm (publication) • Provide recognition for technical/scientific contributions
3. Collegial Maintenance of Standards	• Peer/group evaluation and appraisals • Establishment of appropriate evaluational criteria
4. Autonomy	• Reduce the network rules/regulations for professionals • Protective structures (professional liaisons) • Use of time and funds for personal goals • Removal from physical plant to smaller "garage"-type environments, or "independent business units," to induce creativity and innovation • Freedom to select tasks and projects and to implement one's own ideas; flexible working hours • Delete "tight" supervisory controls • Delegate decisionmaking authority
5. Commitment to Calling	• Establish alternative promotional ladders to allow technical professionals to remain in the specialties (with parity) • Career assessment and development
6. External Referents and Identification	• Encourage attendance at professional meetings and research presentations • Publish and take out patents and copyrights under professional's own name

be to avoid obsolescence and to meet the professional's personal needs for continued growth. The quality of facilities and services— for example, space, privacy, and equipment—are judged by professionals to be critical. Also, Government professionals in particular saw facilitative support services as important.

To encourage the strengthening of technical skills and expertise, leaves of absence, seminars, management training, and sabbaticals were all incentives deemed important by professionals. Some firms that are concerned about maintaining the expertise of their technical professionals allocate 15 to 20 percent of those employees' base pay to additional education and training. Ideally, this additional and continuing education would coincide with developmental counseling and "career-shifting." Career-shifting identifies appropriate career movement within a firm's technical or managerial ladders to facilitate an employee's growth and continued development. Professional incentives also include permitting career changes for obsolete professionals whose continued expertise requires different skills and knowledge.

Ethics

Ideally, firms would avoid allowing professionals to experience tremendous role conflict owing to their codes of ethics and client orientation. It should be remembered that the professional's code of ethics may conflict with what the firm sees as acceptable marketing practices. To the professional, those practices may appear to be deceptive marketing of products or services. Further, the firm's claims of ownership of new products, and its need to keep them secret, may also conflict with the professional's ethical stance.

Cognizant of some of the tough choices that the professional needs to make, the firm might ease the ethical tensions by offering the following professional incentives: allowing information-sharing with professional referents outside the firm; allowing professionals to publish the results of their research; and providing recognition for scientific or technical contributions that add to the knowledge base (Von Glinow 1983).

The fact that professionals are more prone than most to ethical ambivalence (Jansen and Von Glinow 1985) creates particularly difficult conflicts. Ethical ambivalence is the conflict of the behaviors, attitudes, and norms that are shaped and reinforced through the organization's reward system with the behaviors, attitudes, and norms that are congruent with the ethical values and judgments of organizational stakeholders. When we realize that reward systems frequently reward the behaviors they are really trying to discourage, while punishing the desired behaviors, we can more easily understand the mixed messages that the professional is receiving. Thus, firms should investigate the organizationally-acceptable norms, attitudes, and behaviors that are ethically problematic for the professional.

Collegial Maintenance of Standards

Given the professional's desire to be evaluated by a collegial group of equals—or by those who are directly involved in the technical aspects of the job—the firm should attempt to downplay the bureaucratic aspects of control systems in favor of the more collegial aspects. An appropriate incentive might be using peer evaluation as the primary performance appraisal to determine whether performance has been achieved. Further, care must be taken in establishing the criteria for evaluating or controlling the performance of professionals. For example, the high-tech employee's direct impact on company sales may be unknown. This knowledge may be necessary to the firm, but it is hardly important to the employee who is more concerned with innovation. Thus, performance criteria must be established that are appropriate and are communicated as such.

Rewarding professional contributions may also mean that the firm must rework old performance appraisal forms to concentrate on those aspects of professional performance that are critical, rather than on those that are secondary. Finally, *who* does the appraisal may be just as important as *what* is being appraised.

Autonomy

As discussed earlier, professional employees should be insulated against the network of rules and regulations that interferes with their demands for autonomy. Some protective structures have been successfully employed to buffer the professional. These structures are akin to "linking pins" and, as discussed in Chapter 10, are referred to as professional "liaisons" (Schriesheim, Von Glinow, and Kerr

1977). Any buffering device is implicitly applying rules and regulations differently to professionals. Since technical specialists often view organizational control systems as interfering with their strategic and operational autonomy, the simple act of buffering that professional can be highly rewarding.

There is new evidence that supports giving the professional incentives that may decrease alienation, such as time off, or funds for personal projects unrelated to organizational goals. Other incentives include giving professionals the freedom to select tasks or projects, the freedom to implement their own ideas, and flexible working hours. The concept of "controlled freedom" is also relevant here. A firm that takes on a more participative role and consults with professionals about assignments and changes is exercising controlled freedom. This concept appears to work best within moderately bureaucratic structures. Employees of too heavily bureaucratized firms will see controlled freedom as incidental or as virtually worthless; whereas professionals in nonbureaucratized firms will see it as somewhat of an intrusion into their autonomy.

Similar to controlled freedom is the concept of removing professionals from the physical plant and allowing them to work within smaller "garage"-type units—"independent business units," or "skunkworks"—which allows them by removing the traditional strictures of most organizational control systems, to be more creative.

Since autonomy can be theatened by organizational measures of performance, by requirements for short-term, quantifiable results, and by the tendency to put professionals on teams, some supervisory controls might be lightened. In this case, the structure of the control system would substitute for the structure of the supervisor. Clearly, allowing professionals more freedom to make decisions, with more authority, is a strong professional incentive.

Commitment to Calling

The most powerful incentive that matches the professional's commitment to the field is the use of dual ladders, or alternate career paths, for those who wish to remain within their technical specialties without foregoing social and organizational indicators of success. Promotion into management has been the usual route for technical professionals interested in advancement. While this move may be appropriate for some, many professionals are so committed to their fields that shifting away from their technical specialty is disastrous. The successful firms that utilize dual ladders—for example, IBM and Hewlett-Packard—have provided incentives and rewards associated with promotion, but without an attendant increase in managerial duties. The purpose here is to ensure equity and power for those on the technical ladder.

As with concerns about autonomy, the firm should consider designing these dual ladders with a certain career-sensitivity. That is, the organization can focus its energies on the design of a career-oriented human-resource system that provides career assessment guidance for its professional and high-technology employees.

External Referents and Professional Identification

Professionals generally resist bureaucratic rules and supervision, reject bureaucratic standards, and have conditional loyalties to the organization. For the most part, their important referents are external to the firm. There is some evidence that providing time, funds, and encouragement to attend professional meetings and present research, results in lower alienation.

One incentive that encourages professionals to align with external sources of identification is permitting them to publish under their own names, not only under the name of the company. Some firms also allow professionals to take out patents and copyrights in their own names and to join professional associations and attend their meetings, for which the firm reimburses the employee for expenses. Some firms even offer bonuses for professional papers accepted at national association meetings or for becoming officers of professional associations. Other firms have discovered that advertising the accomplishments of professionals in the company's newsletter can result in increased organizational commitment and job satisfaction.

Some firms sponsor consortia for idea-sharing purposes. For example, Westinghouse, Combustion Engineering, and Ebasco all work together on a consortium in a foreign market to enhance the quality of the local product. Clearly, the degree to which the primary firm encourages interaction with other skilled professionals or firms correlates strongly with professional orientation. Some research reports that the more organizational prestige professionals have, the greater their organizational commitment and loyalty (Lee 1969).

In general, we know that organizational commitment and loyalty increases with the professional's age, seniority, and tenure. Thus, a firm would be well advised to concentrate on equipping the professional with a strong sense of professional identity early in his or her organizational career, then building upon that identity through career development.

Incentives and rewards as they relate to a firm's culture will be discussed further in Chapter 7.

7 HOW REWARD SYSTEMS SHAPE COMPANY CULTURE

> *Consistent runners-up find their jobs gone.*
> —A PepsiCo manager

> *You have to shoot the president to get fired.*
> —A UPI manager

These two quotations from a *Business Week* article suggest two very different types of corporate cultures and reward systems. The culture of PepsiCo has historically placed great value on competitive success, rewarding winners and ousting losers. Employees in that setting have a reasonably clear set of guidelines about what they must do to merely survive, and what they must do to prosper. The corporate culture of UPI is one of paternalism, and one in which almost anything would be tolerated. Both draw our attention to an important fact of organizational life—that a company's culture and reward system are not only interdependent but they feed off each other. With minor exceptions, this fact has rarely been acknowledged in the management literature (Sethia and Von Glinow 1984; Kerr and Slocum 1987).

The purpose of this chapter is to focus attention on the culture-reward system relationship and to highlight the implications of this relationship for managing high-tech and professional employees.

THE TWIN CONCEPTS

Corporate Culture

Most of us have a somewhat intuitive feel for corporate culture; the subject has captured the attention of practitioners and scholars alike in the 1980s. While there are no absolute definitions of organizational culture, the following offer common themes.

Peters and Waterman (1982) talk about culture as the shared values of the company's members. Kilmann (1982) calls it the "collective will of members . . . indicating what the corporation really wants or what really counts in order to get ahead." Schein (1983) refers to it as the "sum total of the collective or shared learnings of a group." For purposes of discussion, I am using the Sethia and Von Glinow (1985) definition: "Culture is the shared and relatively enduring pattern of basic values, beliefs, and assumptions in an organization" (p. 403).

As described in Chapter 5, "organizational reward system" refers to interrelated elements: the types of rewards that are available, the conditions under which these rewards are made available to members, and the ways in which the rewards and the criteria are administered. If an organization's culture involves the basic values, assumptions, and beliefs of its members, the twin concept is that culture is influential in determining the types of rewards that are available in an organization, the conditions under which the rewards are allocated to groups or individuals, the way in which the rewards and their criteria are selected, and the manner in which the total reward system is administered (Sethia and Von Glinow 1985; Von Glinow 1985).

Often the impact of a firm's culture is quite direct; such an impact can be seen in ruthlessly performance-oriented cultures, such as PepsiCo, where rewards are based solely on certain aspects of performance. A firm's culture can influence its reward system indirectly through its human-resource philosophy and practices. Much of the substance of culture is "concerned with controlling the behaviors and attitudes of organization members, and the reward system is a primary method of achieving control" (Kerr and Slocum 1987: 99). HR philosophies and practices that are sensitive to the high-technology and professional employee underly corporate policies such as "job

Figure 7-1. The Culture-Reward System Relationship.

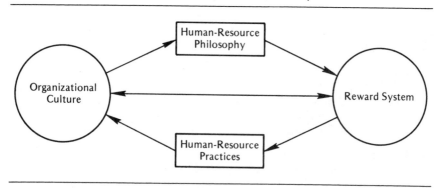

content rewards, peer appraisals, career development, duel ladders and autonomous working environments" (Von Glinow 1985: 194). Firms like IBM, AT&T, and Hewlett-Packard have well-developed HR philosophies—articulated through their credos—that impact the reward practices of these firms.Hewlett-Packard's practices include no layoffs, long-term incentives and rewards, and incentives that are companywide. Figure 7-1 illustrates the relationships between culture and reward systems.

The twin concepts are highly intertwined. Stonich (1984) notes that current culture is a function of past reward policies. Lawler (1983) notes that the reward system can reinforce and help define the organizational structure. That is, the reward system can help define the degree to which technical professionals can influence line management, and it can strongly influence the kind of decisionmaking structure that exists. In short, reward systems can shape culture because they influence motivation, satisfaction, and membership. "The behaviors they cause to occur become the dominant patterns of behavior in the organization and lead to perceptions and beliefs about what an organization stands for, believes in, and values" (Lawler 1983: 11).

Until recently, Chase Manhattan Bank was not particularly performance-driven and "rewarded people more for appearance than performance," which resulted in "inbreeding and a smugness that made the bank loathe to grapple with competitors" (*Business Week* 1980: 158). Thus, a company's culture and its reward system must be in a balanced relationship for the company to function smoothly (Sethia and Von Glinow 1985).

But particular types of organizational cultures appear to function best with particular types of reward systems. The matching combinations fall into four very distinguishable patterns (Sethia and Von Glinow 1985; Von Glinow 1985). These patterns are based on two important positions: the firm's concern about the people in the firm as vital stakeholders; and the intensity of the firm's expectations around member performance. As noted earlier, many firms have HR philosophies that focus on the importance of human assets, whereas others focus on the role that performance plays. Though not interchangeavle, both philosophies represent two very important dimensions of organizational life, which are fundamental to our discussion. Beliefs about people and beliefs about performance underly the following discussion of different cultures and the types of reward systems generally associated with each.

A TYPOLOGY OF DIFFERENT CULTURES

As discussed, the underpinnings of a company's culture are revealed by its human-resource orientation. Therefore, company cultures may be differentiated and classified by examining their concern for human assets and their concern for performance. Concern for human assets refers to the firm's commitment to the well-being of its members and its respect for their values, attitudes, and beliefs. Concern for performance refers to the firm's expectation that its members will give their personal best on their jobs.

We can discern the following typology of organizational cultures: a low or high level of concern for human assets, coupled with a low or high level of concern for performance, suggests four generic types of organizational cultures, which are grounded in the HR orientations of each type (Sethia and Von Glinow 1985). These four types, as shown in Figure 7-2, are the apathetic culture, the caring culture, the exacting culture, and the integrative culture.

The apathetic culture shows relatively little concern for the firm's human assets and indifference to their performance. The caring culture shows high concern for people as assets and has relatively undemanding performance expectations. The exacting culture exhibits little sensitivity to the people of the firm, but has demanding and exacting performance expectations. The integrative culture shows high concern for people and has high performance expectations.

Figure 7-2. Framework of Human-Resource Cultures.

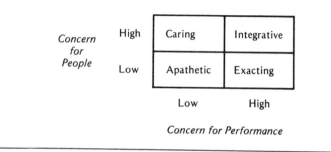

In general—and somewhat contrary to the thinking of Sethia and Von Glinow (1985)—these cultures support a variety of reward systems. Each culture, however, is optimally compatible with only one specific type of reward system. The reward systems that seem to be compatible with each of the four cultures are summarized in Table 7-1.

The Apathetic Culture

Apathetic cultures are inherently counter-rational. Such firms lack concern for people and are indifferent to their performance. Apathetic firms seem to operate in moral vacuums, with inept or alienated leadership. Clearly, the long-term prospects for such firms are problematic; but they may survive if they have a monopolistic position in their industry or are protected by law.

An example of the apathetic culture is the one that prevailed at RCA until recently. According to *Business Week* (1984), in a cover article the company historically was "dominated by Byzantine cabals, factions, and schisms," and during that time, "talk of who was up and who was down occupied the troops far more than the company's business." Apparently, there were reports of "bureaucratic hacks who had built power bases by virtue of long tenure" (p. 53). Top aides were hired and publicly fired, but they were "compensated handsomely both coming in and going out" (p. 54). Some analysts suggested that the denigration of people and the neglect of performance for so many years literally drained the vitality of this pioneer in radio and television.

Table 7-1. Compatibility of Reward Systems with Four Cultures.

	Human-Resource Cultures			
Reward Systems	Apathetic	Caring	Exacting	Integrative
1. Types of Reward				
Financial	Low	Average	Variable	Excellent
Status	Excellent	Excellent	Moderate	Low
Job Content	Poor	Average	Good	Excellent
Career	Poor	Good	Average	Excellent
Professional	Poor	Average	Good	Excellent
2. Sample Criteria for Reward				
Performance: results	Individual success illusory	Reasonable effort day-to-day	Individual success short-term	Individual/group/ firm success long-term
Performance: actions and behaviors	Manipulation; politicking	Compliance; cooperation	Efficiency; competition	Innovation; independence
Nonperformance considerations	Contract; patronage	Member; position	Nature of work; costs of replacement	Equity; potential

Source: Adapted from Nirmal Sethia and Mary Ann Von Glinow, "Arriving at Four Cultures by Managing the Reward System," in Kilmann, Saxton, Serpa and Associates, ed., *Gaining Control of the Corporate Culture* (San Francisco: Jossey-Bass, 1985).

While there are other reported examples of apathetic cultures, they are not as common among high-tech businesses operating in highly competitive environments with narrow profit margins. Instead, this culture is more apt to be found in strong monopolies, cartels, some public-sector organizations, and state-owned enterprises in some countries. In these types of organizations, entrenched interests prevail, as do political expediencies and ideological proclivities.

An examination of the reward strategies used to attract, motivate, and retain high-tech and professional workers reveals that apathetic firms offer a considerable amount of job security. In some cases, lucrative contracts are offered. To attract qualified professionals, these types of companies rarely use the term "performance-oriented," but instead rely on matters of custom ("We've always done it that way") or on patronage (Von Glinow 1985). Since the company perceives that it has no real competition, the recruiting pitch may not focus on productivity. Knowing that a firm is not terribly bottom-line–driven can appeal to some high-tech and professional workers. This environment may appeal to those who are not risk-oriented, or to those who do not really care to work on product innovations that must meet some competitive standard or be held up to strict scrutiny.

In this type of culture, financial rewards are generally poor to average, although in some cases, as mentioned above, the financial rewards may be more generous. Job content rewards seem relatively difficult to come by in this type of company. Career rewards—principally job security—are high, but promotions are generally slow. Growth opportunities appear rather limited. Status rewards are usually limited to a privileged few and are highly visible.

To retain professionals in this culture, strategies revolve around showing professionals how they may capitalize upon the absence of certain factors (for example, lack of performance standards or competitive threats). This culture may appeal to those professionals and high-tech workers who are more politically oriented or power-driven than others, since the ability to play politics and hide behind the "rules" is its own reward (Von Glinow 1985). Professional rewards, however, like job content rewards, are generally missing; the commitment that professionals have to their specialty is not particularly valued in the apathetic culture.

Since, by definition, performance is not deemed important, most rewards are likely to come from meeting one's contractual obligations, or from patronage. Some individuals may use what they perceive as their personal accomplishments to bargain for rewards, although such accomplishments are generally more illusory than real. Actions and behaviors that pay off include politicking, manipulating rules, and the like.

The Caring Culture

Like the apathetic culture, the caring culture has weak performance expectations of its professionals. This culture, however, is very concerned about its employees; its attitude can border on the paternalistic. The traditional cultures of firms like AT&T, Bank of America, and Corning Glass are representative of this type of culture. As long as the environment poses no real competitive threat, these firms can function quite smoothly, since employees readily comply with organizational leaders. The people may be said to be extremely loyal.

The types of rewards that are available to attract, motivate, and retain professionals generally play up the "human side of the company [as exhibited] through its management practices" (Von Glinow 1985: 198). These companies highlight job security, career rewards, and the sense of working for a firm that is trustworthy and fair. In general, training and development programs within these cultures are good. Status rewards tend to be substantial, but as with the apathetic culture, job content and professional rewards tend to be on the low end. Financial rewards tend to be average, by market standard. To attract professionals, the caring culture company offers incentives such as geographical location, a good school district, and child-care facilities. In addition, some front-end bonuses are given.

Given the trend toward dual-career families, it should be noted that most of the rewards offered by caring cultures tend to focus on individual professional needs. If these companies have attracted professionals who do not want intrusions into their autonomy, they need to offer some degree of autonomy to motivate such professionals to stay.

Retention is a key concern, and these firms frequently engage their professional staff in attitude and morale surveys. Also, opportunities for training and development are common, as are programs designed to upgrade skills and education. Caring companies also try to retain professionals by promoting from within and by using perquisites for those in senior ranks. In addition, we would expect these companies to have strong pension programs and programs that allow professionals to phase-retire if they choose.

Since conditions for rewards are not particularly performance-based—although people are expected to make reasonable efforts in their daily work—some actions and behaviors are more likely than others to influence the employee's rewards. For example, teamwork, cooperation, conformity, and "playing it safe" would be rewarded. Similarly, politicking, manipulation, and taking risks would not be rewarded.

Many rewards in the caring culture are membership-based, while other rewards are governed mainly by tenure and position in the firm's hierarchy. The personnel policies of Bank of America have been labeled "traditional" and have been likened to those of the civil service; one corporate officer observed that "everybody at a certain grade could expect about the same salary and the same increase" (Zonana 1984: 1).

The Exacting Culture

This is the culture that might be described as "perrformance-driven," or success-oriented. In this cultural pattern, performance is what counts, and individuals are sometimes expendable (Sethia and Von Glinow 1985). Employees are expected to perform at a sustained level of high performance, epitomized by Grove's (1983) description of Intel, where people are expected to do their "personal best."

Some likely possibilities here include PepsiCo, Texas Instruments, ITT during the reign of Geneen, Intel, and Emerson Electric, where nothing is said to be more sacred than the bottom line (*Business Week* 1983).

In these cultures, financial rewards are generally substantial. These include profit-sharing, front-end bonuses, and stock options, coupled with special award and recognition bonuses associated with successful performance. The exacting culture makes a point of "being Number One," of "going for the best." Emerson Electric, for example, rewards superachievers handsomely. "Divisional managers can increase their annual compensation up to 81 percent by exceeding preset goals" (*Business Week* 1983: 61).

Job content and professional rewards can be high in the exacting culture because the professional must utilize exceptional expertise and skill in meeting and exceeding performance expectations. While status rewards vary from company to company, there is prestige associated with being with the best firm. Job security tends to be low, and other career rewards are moderate, since a professional's security is strictly dependent upon how well he or she performs. This results-oriented emphasis precludes meaningful employee development programs, thus contributing to rapid burnout (Sethia and Von Glinow 1985).

The availability of rewards in the exacting culture is highly contingent upon the results of the professional's efforts. Also, the short-term emphasis generally outweighs any long-term focus. The types of actions and behaviors that pay off tend to be predicated on success. Almost anything goes, as long as it is successful. Hoarding of resources, withholding information, and not taking risks may be rewarded—as long as these actions and behaviors produce successful results. Taking risks and being innovative and creative are ostensibly rewarded in this culture; however, they can be discouraged by the penalties associated with failure. Nonperformance criteria generally do not determine the rewards in the exacting culture.

The Integrative Culture

This culture category matches high concern for people with strong performance expectations. The net result is a blend of values; professionals are considered capable of significant contributions to the overall goals of the firm, as well as to their own goals. The integrative culture appears to offer above-average rewards of all types—with the exception of status rewards—to attract, motivate, and retain high-technology and professional employees. The integrative culture values people and attempts to challenge them in meaningful ways.

IBM, Hewlett-Packard, and Tandem Computers fit this culture category. Employees are considered capable of making significant contributions to these firms and are expected to do so. The performance expectation is not paternalistic or demanding, but concentrates on the dignity of people. At Hewlett-Packard, for example, they "recruit the best talent from the best engineering schools . . .

[and] move young engineers quickly into significant jobs in an informal environment" (*Business Week* 1982: 78).

Available rewards include offering professionals well–above-average compensation and benefits to initially attract and subsequently retain them. In addition, profit-sharing, stock options, and bonuses are commonly used. Unlike any of the other cultures, professional rewards that link the professional's abilities and expertise to the mission of the firm are well-known.

Integrative firms think about the subsequent training, development, or education that the professional will need. These companies typically promise appropriate career movement (whether in a managerial or a technical specialty) that is predicated on meeting or exceeding company goals. Enlarged jobs and considerable job responsibility are offered to attract professionals who are known to thrive on challenges that are neither too hard nor too easy to achieve (Von Glinow 1985).

Performance is a core value in the integrative culture; thus, significant rewards are contingent upon performance. Performance may be expected of the individual, the group, or the firm, depending on the nature of the jobs. Performance is not viewed, however, solely "in terms of the current bottom line, but long-term implications are also taken into consideration. Actions and behaviors that are valued in the Integrative culture include self-management, cooperation, risk taking, innovation, experimentation and skill building" (Sethia and Von Glinow 1985: 415). Nonperformance rewards may be given for equity purposes or for individual potential.

STRATEGIC IMPLICATIONS FOR REWARD SYSTEM DESIGN

Table 7-2 presents the combinations of reward strategies that typify each of the four categories of culture.

Not all high-tech firms employing professionals will fit neatly into one of the four categories. Further, a firm may encompass subcultures that resemble one of the four categories while the overall firm resembles a different category. Thus, multiple reward systems can coexist in a given culture category. The purpose of culture categorization is to isolate some of the strategic implications involved in the

Table 7-2. Reward Strategies for Organizational Cultures.

Culture	Attraction/Motivation	Retention
Apathetic	No bottom-line emphasis Job security Contracts Matters of custom; patronage Personality; risk-averse	Concentrate on job security and autonomy Appeal to the politically oriented professionals
Caring	People-oriented; job security Trustworthiness and fairness Flexible benefits	Training and development programs Continuing education programs Liberalization of retirement benefits Seniority or tenure-based rewards
Exacting	Financial rewards Bonuses Job content rewards Performance- and success- driven	Profit-sharing Stock ownership Emphasis on entrepreneurial spirit Garage-type independent business units
Integrative	Above-average compensa- tion and benefits Job security Job content rewards Quick advancement opportunities	Skill-based pay Advancement opportunities readily available Tailor-made Challenging Task-relevant feedback

Source: Adapted from Mary Ann Von Glinow, "Reward Strategies for Attracting, Evaluating, and Retaining Professionals," *Human Resource Management* 24, no. 2 (Summer 1985). © 1985 by John Wiley & Sons, Inc.

design of reward systems. The culture categories permit a somewhat deeper analysis and understanding of the organizational realities associated with the employment of professionals.

Therefore, the following implications can be drawn:

1. Culture change requires a change in the reward system. Given that multiple reward systems may coexist in any given culture, it is useful to determine a priori which rewards the culture best supports. Since most high-tech firms engage in culture change to meet competitive threats, it is vital to assess what kinds of rewards and what levels of rewards will best support the desired culture. Reward system change is an integral part of culture change. Given the different forces behind culture change—including changes in company strategy, technology, work values, leadership, and regulatory policy, all discussed in Chapter 2—a parallel change in the company's reward system enhances the likelihood that the culture change will be successful.

2. *Changes involving the reward system must account for the unique role of the professional and high-technology employee.* The salience of rewards has long been a factor in attracting, motivating, and retaining professional employees. Different reward systems should be seriously considered (Von Glinow 1985), particularly in any reward system change effort.

3. *Reward system design should be tailored to specific cultures and organizational situations.* The tailoring of any system does not occur in a vacuum, but rather, resembles aiming at a moving target. As such, it may discourage systematic diagnosis and design. But there are numerous cases where some very innovative reward systems failed to impact organizational performance simply because they did not fit the culture of the firm. System designers should take a critical look at the existing culture to determine if and how the culture is desirable. Given the peculiarities of the different cultures, care should be taken to match the professional with the cultural setting and the reward system. Changes in strategic reward system design argue for more fluid change approaches, as discussed in detail in Chapter 11.

8 TESTS OF A PERFORMANCE-REWARD SYSTEM

In Chapter 6, I discussed the performance-reward relationship and the role that reward systems play in motivating the professional and high-technology employee to perform. The premise was that, if you want the employee to perform, he or she must be rewarded for performing. To accurately reward a professional, performance must be measured properly. Further, system designers should define performance precisely if the measurement device is to work. Finally, employees need feedback about their performance.

The purpose of this chapter is to discuss in greater detail why the rewards judged by professionals and high-tech workers to be most salient are systematically different from traditional rewards employed by most firms to motivate and retain professionals. For this type of analysis, we must determine whether the reward system is actually doing what it was intended to do. That requires a test of the performance-reward system. This text examines the extent to which the various combinations of rewards have been properly combined to attract new employees, to motivate and retain existing employees, to orient the performance of professionals toward organizational goals, and finally, to recognize an employee's successful acceptance of greater accountability and responsibility.

As mentioned in Chapter 6, the most important sources of attraction, motivation, and retention—according to empirical investigation—are the professional rewards associated with the work itself, the career development process, and the organizational processes employed. Notably absent were financial rewards. Nevertheless, any reward system includes a certain number of financial rewards. It is likely that even if the job was filled with great challenge, responsibility, and importance—and the professional's reaction to the work itself was excellent—if the financial reward was dismal, a certain amount of discontent would surface. Therefore, any test of a reward system should systematically examine all of the salient rewards as to their impact on increasing organizational performance.

TESTS OF AN EFFECTIVE REWARD SYSTEM

Chapter 6 initiated the analysis, which began with asking which rewards are attractive to professionals, how the distribution of those rewards is controlled, and what they are contingent upon. Figure 8-1 portrays these questions, within the diagnostic framework discussed earlier. Notice that all categories of rewards—including financial rewards, status rewards, job content rewards, career rewards, and professional rewards—are represented in this organizational diagnostic in the middle column.

A high-tech firm's diagnosis of which combination of rewards best reflects its goals is a "reward system profile" (Kerr 1988), which will be discussed shortly. System designers should concern themselves first with a series of nine key questions, which are tests that the performance-reward system should successfully pass. If the firm is reasonably successful in passing these tests, it is likely that the firm's overall reward system is functioning smoothly, and that goal congruence has been achieved to a reasonable extent.

The Desirability Test

To what extent do key people agree about which goals are important and about which activities are desirable or undesirable?

If key people do not agree about goals, how then will goals be adequately communicated to professional workers? This test reveals the extent to which goals are recognized as important by the crucial stakeholders and whether consensus exists. If we keep in mind the

Figure 8-1. Diagnostic for Organizational Reward Systems.

How Controlled	Incentive/Reward	Contingent Upon
Company policy	Financial Rewards	Individual performance
	Sizable pay increases	
Top management	Stock options	Group performance
	Profit-sharing	
HR division	Vacation time	Attendance
Union	Status Rewards	Variable membership
	Private office	
Immediate superior	Private parking space	Fixed membership
	Access to managerial lounge,	
Self	cafeteria, etc.	Automatically by
		promotion
Subordinate	Job Content Rewards	
	Performance feedback	Personal Factors
Automatically	Job challenge	
over time	Responsibility	Don't know
	Interesting tasks	
Other		Impossible
	Career Rewards	
No one	Job security	
	Career development	
	Dual ladders	
	Professional rewards	
	Continuing education	
	Autonomy	
	Intellectually stimulating projects	
	Opportunity to work with top	
	professionals	

difficulty of achieving goal congruence, we can see that it is not motivation per se but agreement on which goals are the most important that causes problems. Miller (1986) reminds us that agreement on goals and mission is vital, and that if some goals are not "bought" by a segment of the firm, they may be actively thwarted or blocked. This is particularly problematic in managing high-tech and professional employees because it is hard to define all the necessary activities when pursuing unknown goals (Miller 1986).

Having a mission supports the professional's sense of commitment, meaningfulness, and purpose. A firm's goals and mission may well be one reason why the professional was attracted to it in the first place. Thus, organizational goals shape the development of the firm and of the individuals within that firm. For example, there was no agreement at IBM on which goals were important to the firm. Initially, IBM had sold data-processing equipment and services to companies, not to individuals. To enter the personal computer (PC) market—which is very consumer-oriented—IBM needed to redefine its mission and revise the way goals had been established over the course of many years. There was considerable controversy over the decision to enter the PC market because, with minor exceptions, IBM had never sold directly to the individual consumer before.

Therefore, if the reward system is to accurately reward goal attainment by professionals, the key people must agree on which goals are considered important.

The Availability Test

To what extent are the rewards perceived as attractive available to a firm's professionals?

Financial incentives are frequently not available to professionals—because they are not cost-free! Social status incentives may be somewhat more available; however, there are usually only so many window offices to go around. Job content, career, and professional rewards are generally more available than financial or social status rewards.

The relative availability of rewards needs to be discussed by those concerned with linking rewards to performance. Some rewards may be available, but not communicated by managers to subordinates or by the HR function to the firm at large. Key contributor programs have been indicted on this score; the rewards seem to be available, yet no one is interested in claiming them.

The Performance-Contingency Test

To what extent are the rewards performance-related?

Theoretically, professionals are rewarded when they perform; the reward is withheld if they do not perform. In the case of pay, there are only three basic determinants; what job the professional is doing, how long he or she has performed it, and how well he or she has

Figure 8-2. Performance Contingency and the Impact on Performance of Across-the-Board Pay Incentives.

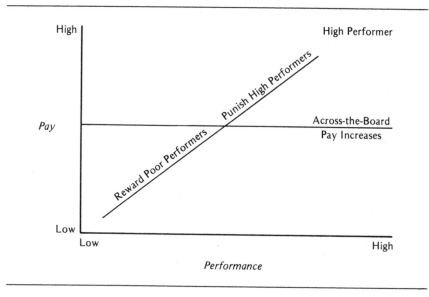

done it. Recently, firms in the United States have shifted away from performance-contingency standards of compensation to treating everyone the same, often with what may be equivalent to across-the-board pay raises. When that occurs, the performance-reward relationship has been violated, and the reward system has failed the performance-contingency test. If there are fewer financial incentives available, particularly in recessionary years, it makes little or no sense to spread them out evenly. In so doing, you punish great performers and reward poor performers. Figure 8-2 displays this relationship:

A related problem has to do with allocating benefits. As of the late 1980s, the single largest benefit that firms have been paying out is compensation to workers for "unused" leave. This means, in effect, paying workers *not to work!* Such payouts clearly fail the performance-contingency test.

The Timeliness Test

To what extent are rewards distributed in a timely manner after performance occurs?

This does not sound too difficult; however, many financial rewards come only once a year, or every six months. To motivate the employee, the reward ideally should be given immediately after the performance. Many financial and social status rewards fail miserably in their motivational purpose because they cannot be administered in a timely fashion.

The "time span of discretion"—the amount of time that it takes for poor performance to show—is relevant here. If the professional performs poorly and the supervisor lets him or her know six months later, the time span of discretion has been violated. Similarly, if the professional has an overly controlling boss who constantly "corrects" work even before mistakes have occurred, the time span of discretion has also been violated. For rewards to have motivational or retentive effects on professionals, the timeliness test should be met.

The Understandability Test

To what extent is the performance appraisal system clearly understood by organization members?

Too frequently for high-technology and professional employees, the performance appraisal process is neither understood nor linked to any meaningful outcomes. Kerr (1988) has maintained that the reward system is only as good as the performance appraisal upon which it rests. Thus, performance appraisal must be understood. This necessity will be discussed further in Chapter 9; however, the relevant point here is that rewards must be visible to be understood. Many so-called rewards are not well understood because they are highly invisible. Benefits actually account for forty cents of every dollar spent today on employees. But since they are generally invisible, benefits tend not to be well understood—thus failing the understandability test.

The "Basic" Test

To what extent are desired activities on the part of the professional and high-technology employee rewarded, and undesirable activities punished?

The discussion in earlier chapters highlights this issue. For the reward system to be doing its job of linking rewards to performance, there should be a clear message to all that performance is rewarded and nonperformance is punished. This becomes tricky when, for example, a professional narrowly misses a very difficult goal or target. Is the employee rewarded for a "good effort," or punished for missing the target?

The "basic" test asks system designers to concentrate on identifying which goals are deemed so important that they can remain unmet only at the professional's peril. Similarly, the firm should become clear on how important it is to punish failure. Very little has been said thus far about punishment, but generally speaking, it has a short-lived effect on altering performance.

The "Who Controls" Test

Are rewards controlled at the proper level and position?

If all rewards are meted out by the personnel department on a highly predictable cycle, the firm fails the test of who best controls the distribution of rewards. For hierarchical superiors to control the performance of their professional and high-tech staffs, they must be able to give rewards for performance attainment. Job content and professional rewards typically fare best on the "who controls" test, while the other categories do worse. It is generally easy to give recognition for a job well done. But it is less easy to give a cash bonus to reward performance, on an as-needed basis.

The Differentiation Test

To what extent does the distribution of rewards accurately and equitably reflect differences in people's performance?

If little differentiation is made, then high performers and low performers will, in essence, be rewarded similarly. When that occurs, the high performer is likely to downgrade his or her performance, in view of the inequity in rewards.

Equity theory taught us years ago that people have a tendency to evaluate their own contibutions in terms of the contributions of others doing similar jobs or tasks. If employees perceive inequity, they are likely to readjust their efforts or contributions to bring their perceptions of performance into alignment. For a reward system to accurately link performance with rewards, it must differentiate between good performers and poor performers in a visible, timely, and meaningful fashion.

The Integration Test

Are the goal-setting, appraisal, feedback, and reward systems highly integrated?

Goal-setting should not be undertaken apart from the appraisal system (Von Glinow, Driver, Brousseau, and Prince 1983). When it comes time for performance appraisal, it should be conducted with explicit, predetermined goals in mind. The parts of any HR system must be connected and well communicated to professionals.

A worksheet version of these tests of a reward system appears at the end of this chapter.

PROFILES OF THE PERFORMANCE-REWARD RELATIONSHIP

As reported in Kerr (1988), the ARS group has developed a series of profiles of healthy and unhealthy reward systems, based upon the reward system diagnostic. These profiles help us visualize what the data reveal, though our images remain somewhat blurred (Kerr 1988).

An Unhealthy High-Tech Firm

Figure 8–3 is a profile of a hypothetical high-tech firm. (In general, the rewards diagnostic requires separate profiles for each unit or level; however, to the extent that similarities occur, they may be jointly constructed.) For illustration, Figure 8–3 shows a firm in which almost all the rewards come from one's membership in the firm, and in which the immediate superior is powerless to influence rewards.

Figure 8-3. An Unhealthy High-Tech Firm.

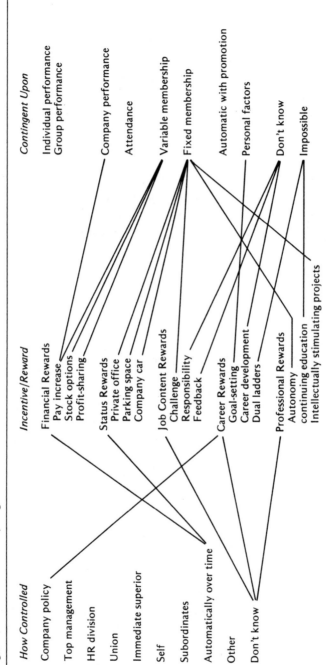

In this company, professionals are not generally rewarded for performance; instead, their rewards stem from how long they have been employed and from the level they have reached. Notice that all financial rewards—with the exception of pay increases, which appear to be contingent upon firm-level performance and not upon individual performance—derive from membership. In other words, all the employee must do is show up long enough, and he or she reaps benefits.

Notice further that all status rewards are contingent upon membership. Job content rewards are given for unknown reasons or because of membership; career rewards are either impossible to receive or stem from personal factors. Professional rewards either derive from membership or are impossible to achieve.

The immediate superior is seen as powerless in administering or controlling rewards. Most of the salient rewards are either controlled by company policy or automatically occur over time. In a few instances, professionals do not know who controls the giving of career, professional, or job content rewards.

This firm is labeled "unhealthy" because its employees are receiving rewards for nonperformance. Why should employees continue to perform well, or even at an acceptable level, when they receive rewards anyway? This profile illustrates a typically dysfunctional reward system; the way in which the rewards are distributed gives the employee one less reason to perform. Apathetic firms, or even caring firms, are more apt to fall into this type of profile, although other cultures may certainly experience reward system dysfunctions when rewards are linked to membership more than to performance. Firms with corporate cultures that have strong performance values are more likely to suffer from breakdowns other than those illustrated by this profile (Miller 1986; Schuster 1984).

Goals are not synchronized and employees tend to suffer from morale problems when they realize that company policy controls virtually everything. When superiors have no control over promotions, pay increases, or punishments, they become organizationally emasculated. Morale suffers on this score as well.

In contrast, Figure 8-4 portrays a hypothetical, "healthy" high-tech firm—where there seems to be agreement over goals and over the means by which those goals are attained.

The difference is immediately apparent. Professionals are given rewards because they have met the performance goals, either indi-

Figure 8-4. A Healthy High-Tech Firm.

vidually or in groups. Status rewards are given for membership only, although in one case a company car was given to each member of an engineering department because they had to do a considerable amount of traveling as part of their jobs. Career rewards were given automatically. Job security, on the other hand, was predicated on how well employees performed. Professional rewards were also based on individual or group performance. In this healthy firm, there is a clear linkage between rewards and performance, and the firm is able to successfully pass most of the tests of a reward system. Firms with this type of profile typically report fewer problems with morale, turnover, and the like, which are associated with the more dysfunctional patterns displayed in Figure 8–3.

Where Leadership Plays a Role

Firms with the Figure 8–4 profile do not have emasculated leaders, but rather, leaders who control the mediation of most salient rewards. This control becomes particularly critical when the hierarchical leader does not possess the technical and professional expertise of the specialist. This profile argues strongly for creating structures that allow the hierarchical superior to equitably distribute rewards for jobs well done by technical professionals. The superior needs to have knowledge of the performance, must be able to properly evaluate that performance, and must administer rewards in a timely fashion if excellent performance is to continue. To do this well, superiors must be particularly aware of the subjective and long-term aspects of some projects.

Superiors who tend to be extremely structuring or controlling, even when the situation may not warrant such control, should be reminded that sometimes the professionals' work "substitutes" for hierarchical leadership. The concept of a substitute for leadership was created by Kerr and Jermier (1978) to describe those situations that may actually substitute for or invalidate hierarchical leadership. For example, high-technology employees engage in work so absorbing as to make hierarchical leadership over their work irrelevant to them. Their professional orientation may seriously neutralize the leader's role. Therefore, hierarchical superiors who are responsible for allocating rewards to professionals need to be aware that if the nature of the professional's job all but invalidates the notion of leadership, his or her credibility as a source of rewards may suffer.

Interestingly, the professional employee can control the distribution of some of his or her job content rewards. Even subordinates can contribute to some of these professional rewards. For instance, a subordinate may contribute significantly to a professional's work on intellectually stimulating projects. When either the professional or the professional's subordinate has some degree of control over the distribution of rewards, the hierarchical superior is rendered additionally useless as a source of valued rewards.

In sum, this chapter identified ways to determine if a performance-reward system is functioning properly. The next chapter examines how performance appraisal systems may be designed to enhance or hinder the performance-reward relationship.

TEST OF AN EFFECTIVE REWARD SYSTEM

1. To what extent do key people agree about which goals are important and about which activities are desirable or undesirable?

   Very little _____ To some extent _____ To a great extent _____

2. To what extent are attractive rewards available to organizational members?

   Very little _____ To some extent _____ To a great extent _____

3. To what extent are important rewards performance-related?

   Very little _____ To some extent _____ To a great extent _____

4. To what extent are rewards distributed in a timely manner after performance occurs?

   Very seldom _____ To some extent _____ To a great extent _____

5. To what extent is the performance appriasal system clearly understood by organizational members?

   Very little _____ To some extent _____ To a great extent _____

6. To what extent are desired activities really rewarded and undesired activities really punished?

   Very little _____ To some extent _____ To a great extent _____

7. To what extent do the right managers control the important rewards desired by their subordinates?

   Very little _____ To some extent _____ To a great extent _____

8. To what extent does the distribution of rewards reflect differences in employee performance?

   Very little _____ To some extent _____ To a great extent _____

9. To what extent are the goal-setting, appraisal, feedback, and reward systems integrated?

   Very little _____ To some extent _____ To a great extent _____

IV STRATEGIES AND SYSTEMS FOR ORGANIZATIONAL SUCCESS

9 DESIGNING PERFORMANCE APPRAISAL SYSTEMS FOR HIGH-TECHNOLOGY EMPLOYEES

Several years ago, a study was undertaken at Sun Company on performance appraisal. The summary review of the performance appraisal process revealed this widely held view, voiced by an anonymous manager: "Seldom have so many strived so hard for so long to develop what has become a sophisticated, costly means for demotivating employees" (Deluca, Kitson, and Morris 1985: 1).

That statement puts in context the particularly thorny problem of appraising the performance of high-technology and professional employees. Deluca, Kitson, and Morris (1985) theorized that from a purely rational point of view, most employees are, by definition, average performers. From a psychological point of view, however, most employees feel that they perform above average.

Data collected at Sun Company by Deluca, Kitson, and Morris (1985) illustrate what these researchers call the "80/30 dilemma"—80 percent of us believe that we are in the top 30 percent of performers. In rating their interpersonal skills, for instance, 100 percent of Sun Company employees believed they were "above average"; 60 percent believed they were in the top 10 percent of performers; and 25 percent believed they were in the top one percent. Seventy percent rated themselves in the top 25 percent on leadership skills, whereas only 2 percent rated themselves "below average." Some sense of how "above average" is commonly defined emerged from the data on engineers. All of them—100 percent—believed they were

117

"above average," but in answering another question, fully 86 percent rated themselves in the top 25 percent of performers.

Deluca, Kitson and Morris (1985) concluded that you cannot build a rational system based on "average" really being "above average." Nevertheless, managers of even the most objective performance appraisal systems must account for this nonrational aspect of human nature—the belief that "average" is "above average"—and recognize that, for most people, purely rational appraisal would be a demotivating experience.

Leskin (1984) framed it nicely when he suggested that most people judge themselves by their intentions; others judge them by their behaviors. Thus, most people seem to believe that they are far more skilled at interpersonal relationships, leadership, and performance in general than most performance appraisals reveal.

The question becomes one of giving accurate feedback and evaluation to high-technology and professional employees—who most likely view their performance as better than their superiors view it—while sustaining high levels of motivation to achieve organizational goals. Some writers believe that the appraisal process is inherently flawed and will never work for professionals (Miller 1986). Others believe that however difficult the process may be, there are some fairly sensible approaches to appraising the performance of these workers (Ilgen and Barnes-Farrell 1984; Von Glinow forthcoming; Beer 1981).

The purpose of this chapter is to discuss some of the major problems associated with performance appraisal for technical professionals and to suggest a series of approaches to those problems. For indeed, performance appraisal is possibly management's best tool in controlling human resources and their productivity (Fombrun and Laud 1983).

WHAT IS PERFORMANCE APPRAISAL?

Definitions of performance appraisal abound in the literature. Resnick and Mohrman (1982) maintain that it is a complex process with interrelated elements, intended to "(1) measure performance, (2) motivate employees, (3) improve performance, (4) plan future work, (5) teach employees what they should do, and (6) distribute pay raises" (p. 2). Bittner (1948) identified fourteen questions that helped managers assess employees: how well they were doing on their jobs; how they measured up to the standards needed to produce a high-quality product at a competitive price; what their strengths and weaknesses were; whether or not they fit in with the firm's way of doing things; and finally, if they were getting ahead as quickly and as far as their ability warranted. DeVries et al. (1986) have a fairly practical orientation, suggesting that it is

> a process by which an organization measures and evaluates an individual employee's behavior and accomplishments for a finite time period. Evaluations are typically done annually by the employee's immediate manager. The judgments are often subsequently used to make administrative decisions (e.g., for salary or promotion) that directly affect the employee (p. 2).

It seems relatively clear that performance appraisal is all of the above, cast within the strategic framework of a firm's goals and mission. Toward that end, Fombrun and Laud (1983) provide a human-resource perspective:

> The appraisal system is recognized as the central human resources activity, whose primary functions are to:
>
> 1. Define the specific job criteria against which performance will be measured.
> 2. Accurately measure past job performance.
> 3. Justify the rewards given to individuals, thereby discriminating between high and low performance.
> 4. Define the development experiences the employee needs to both enhance performance in the current job and prepare for future responsibilities (p. 24).

Resnick and Mohrman (1982) sum it up nicely: "Unfortunately, these idiosyncratic purposes often conflict and people with varying expectations participate in the same event" (p. 2). Hence the discomfort associated with doing performance appraisals. Beer (1981) reminds us that our discomfort with performance appraisals may be traced to a series of interpersonal as well as organizational factors. These include, but are not limited to the quality of the superior-subordinate relationship; the skill with which the appraisal is conducted; and the appraisal system itself, including the goals the organization has for it, the administrative system in which it is embedded, and the forms and procedures that make up the process. In the final analysis, it is safe to say that the performance appraisal (PA) is many things to many people.

WHAT ARE THE CRITICAL PA ISSUES?

There are at least two sets of stakeholders with vested interests in the PA process: practitioners and PA experts (DeVries et al. 1986). This section will discuss these two groups separately, to isolate their specific issues.

Issues for Practitioners. The practicing manager and the human-resource professional are concerned with basic questions of system design and must answer questions like the following.

1. What is the organization's reason for doing PA? Resnick and Mohrman (1982) comment that this question is frequently neglected in doing PA; when that happens, the process most likely will not be designed properly. Other key questions here include: What purposes should or can PA serve? (Increasing performance? Improving relationships between superiors and subordinates? Or simply supporting other HR programs, such as salary administration?) Is the impact of the PA worth the time and investment it requires to do it well? (DeVries et al. 1986).

2. What characterizes effective PA systems? This question rests on two separate issues. What characterizes "effectiveness"? Is there one best way to ascertain this? On the first issue, DeVries et al. (1986) ask whether effectiveness depends on specifying certain outcomes, or if some general approaches (for example, Management-by-Objectives [MBO]) are more effective than others. Implicit in the second question is another: Is there one best method for measuring effectiveness, or should a variety of methods be used, depending upon the employee group? Who is best suited to evaluate the employee's performance? (DeVries et al. 1986: 5). Further, does the PA system have top-management support?

3. What is the appropriate mix of design elements? The practitioner must make choices about the content and the process of the appraisal. Resnick and Mohrman (1982) pose the following questions, covering most aspects of those choices: Which scoring method should be used? What is discussed during the appraisal session? Who contributes information for the evaluation? Who completes the PA form, and when? Who decides upon the criteria for evaluation? Is there an appeal process? What training, if any, needs to be done to support the PA system?

4. What is the relationship of PA to other organizational system elements? To what extent is the PA system fully integrated with other HR functions, including the reward system, training, compensation and salary administration, the legal system, and so forth? Is PA an important communication or signaling device to others in the firm about meeting goals and targets? Can or should the PA system be changed to reflect the organization's needs in a more appropriate fashion? What is the best way to introduce the PA system to engender enthusiasm on the part of employees?

5. What will the role of the PA be in the future? Will PA change as a result of changing demographic and employment trends? If certain types of employees are in short supply, should PA be more leniently applied—or discontinued altogether for these people?

Issues for Experts. The other primary class of stakeholders are the PA experts (Devries et al. 1986). Expert concerns include matters pertaining to the validity and reliability of the instruments for measuring performance. DeVries et al. (1986) reviewed the literature for a twenty-year period and highlighted the following three questions that experts generally raise:

1. What is the impact of involving the evaluated person directly in the PA process? Will the employee react favorably or unfavorably if he or she is encouraged to participate in the PA process?

2. Can an optimal PA form be created to evaluate employees on only the performance-relevant factors? Can rating scales be more appropriately designed to be maximally useful?

3. How can PA be made more bottom-line–focused? Can objective criteria be applied to assess whether the employee accomplished results that are important to the firm?

Together, the practitioners' issues and the experts' issues constitute the playground for PA research and practice. DeVries et al. (1986) note that the experts' issues fall largely within a small subset of the practitioners' issues; this would account for PA research seeming incidental to most practitioners, who are concerned with broader issues.

PA FOR PROFESSIONALS

It is against this backdrop that the special case of professionals is now discussed. It is critical that organizations have an effective PA system for professional and high-tech workers. Drucker (1980) points out that the professional knowledge worker is responsible for economic and social innovation—and thus for productivity—at many firms. These employees are the gatekeepers of important new knowledge, the designers of new products and systems, the drivers of productivity and profitability (Newman and Hinrichs 1980). Since these positions typically represent a significant investment on the part of the firm, they have a high risk potential as well as a high payoff potential. Management of these positions requires careful attention to accurately assessing performance. That is where PA fits in (Newman and Hinrichs 1980).

The PA process for professionals should be designed with the culture of the firm in mind. There really is no "one best way" of designing PA systems for professionals. System designers should carefully weigh the strengths and weaknesses of the "design elements" to determine their impact on the context and goals of the PA system (Resnick and Mohrman 1982). While there is no one best way to design a PA system for professionals, certain design elements may accomplish the goals more effectively than others. For example, designers interested in providing recognition and support for effective performance may choose a system that requires employee input (Mohrman 1981). Designers who are interested in motivating performance improvements may choose a goal-setting approach (Latham and Yukl 1975). Or, designers who wish to allocate scarce funds may choose a ranking system, which actually forces a distribution of performance scores (Cummings and Schwab 1973). Finally, designers who want to emphasize subordinate development may choose a behavior observation approach that allows the manager and the subordinate to jointly identify weaknesses in subordinate performance (Latham and Wexley 1981).

Thus, there may be many goals that the system designers should carefully weigh when they implement a PA system. Once established within a firm, the system is likely to reinforce the actions or behaviors it was designed to assess. It may, however, actually hamper the attainment of some goals. When we consider the special characteristics of the professional and high-technology employee, and some of the fundamental dilemmas in managing these valued people, the PA process becomes critical. Implicit in the process of evaluating these workers are new questions: What aspects of the professional's performance should be evaluated? Who should evaluate that performance? How should it be evaluated?

What to Evaluate

In identifying and choosing the performance criteria, the manager should first decide what aspect or aspects of the professional's performance should be evaluated (Newman and Hinrichs 1980). These criteria generally fall into three discrete categories, which, because most PA systems are designed to measure each employee's job-related performance, are individually based: individual personality traits, behaviors, and outcomes (DeVries et al. 1986: 29). These three categories represent the "measurable domain of individual job performance" (p. 29) and are illustrated in Figure 9-1. DeVries et al. (1986) note that since the "true domain" of job performance is approximate, it is shown as a dotted circle; the other three circles represent the traits, behaviors, and outcomes of the professional's performance.

Job-Related Traits. These are personality characteristics that frequently appear as relevant criteria. They might include characteristics such as initiative, creativity, or leadership ability. These criteria have pluses and minuses associated with them, and these will be discussed later.

Job-Related Behaviors. These criteria tend to be anchored in specific behavioral statements: for example, "She responds quickly to project feedback"; "He works with his subordinates to develop them"; "She works with customers to consider their complaints."

Figure 9-1. Measurable Domain of Individual Performance.

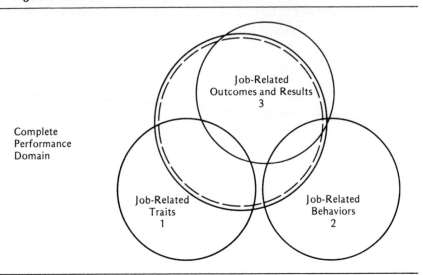

Source: David DeVries, Ann Morrison, Sandra Shullman, and Michael Gerlach, *Performance Appraisal on the Line* (Greensboro, N.C.: Center for Creative Leadership Publication, 1986), p. 29.

Job-Related Outcomes and Results. These criteria may be cost-related: for example, sales volume or quantity of units produced. In general, outcomes are a result of the professional's effort and performance. Other examples might include: "She reduced turnover by 12 percent"; or, "He increased net sales by 10 percent."

The relative success of the PA rests on the extent to which job performance criteria may be accurately specified (DeVries et al. 1986). Each of the three content areas mentioned focuses on different aspects of the performance domain and requires a different measuring approach. As mentioned, this depends on the goals of the system designers and on what they wish to emphasize.

Table 9-1 identifies strengths and weaknesses associated with the measurement instruments designed to measure the performance of professionals and high-technology employees, within the three primary areas of traits, behaviors, and outcomes.

Once identified, these criteria must be measured. Most aspects of a professional's job performance, however, are not objectively measurable. If that were not the case, then measurement issues would disappear as a concern in appraising the performance of professionals.

Table 9-1. Strengths and Weaknesses of Performance Appraisal Instruments for High-Tech and Professional Employees.

Performance Instruments	Strength	Weakness
Traits (e.g., initiative, creativity, loyalty)	Can be developed quickly Can be used across jobs Are highly relevant in initial selection process	Poorly suited to feedback for professionals Often rejected by the courts
Behavior Criteria (e.g., responds to memos quickly; smiles at customers)	Can be related more directly to what a professional actually does Specifies what professionals must do to produce cost-related outcomes Well-suited to performance feedback and goal-setting Courts tend to accept their content-validity	Take a long time to develop Must be developed on a job-to-job basis Difficult to determine for professionals involved in innovation and creativity Very expensive to develop
Outcomes (e.g., sales volume, units of production)	May be good indicators of organizational effectiveness Appeal to senior-level management, venture capitalists, and stockholders	Ignore other important areas of the professional's performance Difficult to obtain from many kinds of professionals Ignore factors professionals cannot control Poorly suited for feedback May take up to three years to track

As with most other jobs, however, it is difficult to get objective performance data for professionals (Landy and Farr 1980). We must assume then that job performance can be defined and observed to such an extent that we may assess it, even though we may have difficulty measuring it (Patten 1977).

It is not uncommon for highly subjective judgment calls to enter into the discussion of assessing the professional's performance, given the ambiguities associated with the innovation and creativity processes. When these judgment calls are used—and they dominate the vast majority of PA measures (DeVries et al. 1986)—the PA measurement process becomes susceptible to problems of rater accuracy, credibility, and dependability. To address rater accuracy, system designers must now concern themselves with psychometric and legal guidelines. The following discussion briefly highlights the key issues (Smith 1976; Newman and Hinrichs 1980; DeVries et al. 1986).

Validity. The core of the measurement issue is validity—the relationship the performance measures have with job performance. Are the measures measuring what was intended to be assessed? Given that some group or person has established that some activities are more important to success than others, the system designer must develop psychometrically sound measures of those activities. Three types of validity are addressed in the PA literature:

1. *Criterion-related validity.* This type of validity involves the degree to which the measures of performance predict relevant elements in the expected job performance. As we have noted, the measures of performance for professionals may be suspect; therefore, this type of validity may have limited application in appraisals for professionals and high-tech workers.

2. *Construct validity.* This describes the extent to which a specific PA measurement technique assesses a specific characteristic that is judged to be important to job performance (traits, behaviors, outcomes). Traits have been frequently employed as constructs for measuring the performance of professionals. Their use is suspect, since no validation procedure is universally accepted (DeVries et al. 1986).

3. *Content validity.* This type of validity refers to how well the performance criteria represent the job content (DeVries et al. 1986). In general, this type of validity requires us to ask whether

all aspects relevant to job performance are represented in the content sampled.

Reliability. Related to validity is the concept of reliability. This refers to the stability and consistency of the measurement results. Measurement results are considered reliable if they are stable across rating periods and are consistent from one rater to another (Smith 1976; Wexley 1979; DeVries et al. 1986). When instabilities or inconsistencies arise in the measurement results, they are often attributed to "noise" in the system or to rater "error," which is to suggest that there is a one best way of assessing reliability and that all raters have similar knowledge of the professional's performance. The difficulty for professionals working on long-term, ambiguous projects is obvious.

Usefulness. Here we are concerned with how relevant or useful the measurement results are in accomplishing the PA purposes. Newman and Hinrichs (1980) also refer to this as "practicality": How plausible is the performance measurement as a tool for making decisions? We know that the results of the PA are put to a variety of uses, and that each use places unique demands on the measurement device (DeVries et al. 1986). We also know that a measurement strategy may be valid and reliable, but fail to meet its intended uses. Thus, the "usefulness" aspect also plays a critical role in measuring the performance of professionals and high-tech workers.

Multidimensionality. Particularly for professionals, using a single measure of job performance success is highly unlikely to provide meaningful PAs. Performance for these people is typically defined in many ways, including technical competence and risk-taking. It stands to reason that it is important to assess all dimensions considered relevant and useful to performance.

Discriminability. Does the PA measurement approach accurately tap differences in employee performance? For professionals, who do a myriad of jobs in research settings, the measurement approach should be able to discriminate between employees as to their levels of performance. When there are only highly subjective measures, the evaluator may suffer from leniency, "central tendency," or harshness in evaluating the professional's performance. ("Leniency" implies that a "soft" standard is used; "central tendency" refers to a general clustering of all employees' performances around the midpoint of the scale; and "harshness" refers to rating the professional's performance low, with all scores clustering around the low end of the instrument.) Ideally, the measurement strategy would accurately discriminate between all types of performance, with as little rater bias as possible.

Who Should Evaluate

In most organizational settings that include high-technology and professional employees, the immediate superior is responsible for the performance evaluation. Because of some of the problems associated with expertise and autonomy, however, that choice may not be appropriate (Smith 1976; Newman and Hinrichs 1980; Von Glinow forthcoming). It has been noted in Chapter 3 that the hierarchical superior may lack the competence, time, or ability to observe the job performance. When that happens, the hierarchical superior may not have a valid, credible, or trustworthy basis for evaluation. The credibility of the source giving the performance feedback has been documented as a major factor influencing the acceptance of that feedback (Ilgen, Fisher, and Taylor 1979).

Two factors appear to be important in determining the credibility of the superior as an evaluator of the performance of the professional: the superior's expertise and his or her trustworthiness. Some have gone so far as to say that it is the quality of the rater, rather than the form or technique employed, that is most important (Bayroff, Haggerty, and Rundquist 1954). Some studies have revealed that research labs headed by technical specialists come up with a greater number of successful innovations. Thus, there is a strong correlation between the productivity of the professional and who does the appraisal.

Expertise. Ilgen, Fisher, and Taylor (1979) suggested that expertise includes familiarity with the task itself, as well as familiarity with the professional's task performance. Von Glinow and Sethia (1983) discovered that those with expertise were generally characterized as knowledgeable, well-informed, and respected. Given the professional's penchant for collegial maintenance of standards, it stands to reason that if the hierarchical superior is also expert in the technical specialty, he or she will be viewed as a more credible source of the performance evaluation. If the immediate superior is not the most expert, or is not the appropriate expert for the specialty, credibility suffers. There are, of course, other options for PA sources that may be considered, including peer evaluations. These will be discussed later.

Trustworthiness. Trustworthiness has also been found to be a major factor that influences how credible the hierarchical superior is to the professional. If the superior is seen as nonthreatening, or not overbearing, and if the professional trusts the superior's motives, then it is more likely that the superior will be seen as a trustworthy source of PAs.

Both expertise and trustworthiness affect the credibility of the hierarchical superior. But other factors appear to affect one's credibility as well. For example, the level of interdependence between the superior and the professional affects how the professional views the superior. Ilgen, Mitchell, and Fredrickson (1981) discovered that the extent to which rewards given by the superior were linked to goal attainment by the subordinate influenced how helpful the superior would be. Greller and Herold (1975) remind us that proximity also affects credibility. If the professional is psychologically close to the hierarchical superior, the superior tends to have greater credibility.

If the immediate superior is not the most appropriate source for conducting the PA, other options, which have been tried with considerable success, can be exercised. Peer ratings tend to be the most popular. Sun Company and ARCO have experimented successfully with peer evaluators; all members of a project or team evaluate one another's performance. When professionals or high-tech workers in a group are performing the same tasks, this can be done fairly easily. Where considerable divergence exists—as in the case of Sun Company, where technicians working on the same oil and gas project were evaluating the performance of the geologists—care should be taken to standardize performance ratings, using as much information on different job dimensions as possible. In a sense, this does not detract from the PA; it enhances the PA by providing multiple raters and multiple dimensions.

Still another option is rating by subordinates. This is a common practice in university settings, where students sometimes evaluate a professor's performance. This type of rating is somewhat problematic; nevertheless, it can be employed successfully. Care should be taken to ensure that neither side feels ill at ease (Morrison, McCall, and DeVries 1978).

A third option includes having professionals rate themselves, in addition to having their superiors rate their performance. There is some evidence that having the professional involved in the process reduces the potential for conflict (Von Glinow forthcoming) and enhances the psychological momentum for a successful PA. When professionals and superiors simultaneously rate the professional's performance and the appraisals are then compared, in cases where little disagreement exists the conflict is diffused before it can begin. Where there are a few disagreements, there can be reasoned focus on those few disagreements, rather than on the entire PA.

Finally, performance may be evaluated by outsiders, such as psychologists or experienced managers trained in evaluation techniques. These evaluations can occur within assessment centers or within inhouse training facilities. Typically, these evaluations have more to do with situational exercises, leadership training, interpersonal interactions, and individual testing (Newman and Hinrichs 1980), rather than with evaluations of technical competence.

Thus, the question of "who should evaluate" the performance of the professional does not always have a clear-cut answer.

PERFORMANCE FEEDBACK
FOR PROFESSIONALS

The question of how to give performance appraisals to professional and high-tech workers requires a discussion of the performance feedback process. Prior to feedback, questions have arisen by practitioners as to whether the performance evaluation should be fed back to the professional at all. If the stated purpose of the PA is to maximize the accomplishment of organizational goals, and there is a discrepancy between expected performance and actual performance, then it is important to inform the professional so that performance may be enhanced in future evaluation periods (Newman and Hinrichs 1980).

Feedback is a critical element of that process. Without feedback, it is all but impossible for the professional to calibrate his or her performance according to the criteria discussed earlier. Feedback has also been judged as essential for learning, directing actions, growth, shaping attitudes, and motivating employees (Ilgen, Fisher, and Taylor 1979; Von Glinow and Sethia 1983). So generally speaking, some feedback is better than no feedback, particularly within high performing systems.

A review of the performance feedback literature for professionals reveals that feedback is usually judged to be effective or not depending upon its outcomes. Typical outcomes might include increased motivation, a change of actions, or increases in productivity. Therefore, in giving a professional feedback about his or her performance, the success or failure of that feedback has usually been predicated on whether the professional was able to change as a result of it. Understanding how to give performance feedback, however, requires more than a post hoc analysis of whether action was taken. Other factors that impact the effectiveness must be addressed. There are three components to the feedback process, and they are not solely limited to examining the outcomes of the feedback: the acceptance phase, the usability of the feedback, and the outcomes of the feedback (Von Glinow and Sethia, 1983).

In the acceptance phase, the professional decides whether to accept or reject the feedback. (See Figure 9–2.) Acceptance or rejection is usually a function of who is doing the appraising, what is being said, and characteristics of the professional. If the feedback is accepted, then the feedback process goes on to next phase: making decisions about action planning in response to the feedback. Is the feedback useful for the professional? This assessment includes issues such as message validity, message specificity, message consistency, and the timeliness of the message. The final phase has to do with how the professional utilizes the feedback, or the outcomes of the feedback. In other words, was direction given? Was the professional more motivated to perform? Did output increase?

It is critically important that the professional accept the feedback initially, and there are a series of measures the firm may employ to enhance the chances of acceptance. There are also institutional measures related to the usability and the outcomes of feedback that have been empirically derived (Von Glinow and Sethia 1983).

Table 9–2 outlines a series of measures that a firm should consider employing to encourage professionals to accept feedback and to change their behavior as a result of it. These suggested measures are

Figure 9-2. The Feedback Process: A Three-Phase Model.

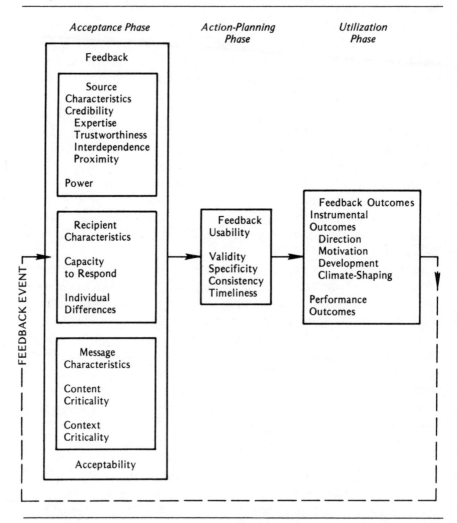

Source: Mary Ann Von Glinow and Nirmal Sethia, in *Producing Useful Knowledge for Organizations*, edited by Kilmann, et al. (copyright © 1983 by Praeger Publishers, New York). Reprinted with permission.

Table 9-2. Criteria for Effective Feedback and Suggested Institutional Measures.

Criteria for Effective Feedback	Suggested Institutional Measures
Acceptance of Feedback	
Source credibility	Select knowledgeable and trustworthy colleagues and practitioners as evaluators and sources of feedback; encourage collaboration and other forms of professional interaction between sources and recipients
Source power	Administer rewards in closer consultation with users and evaluators
Recipient response capability	Give researchers freedom to experiment, retool, learn, and change; allow researchers periodic "time-outs," without enforcing traditional performance criteria
Recipient receptivity	Allow researchers to pursue particular types of research without fear of reprisals
Message importance	Give evaluators detailed information about the work under review and about the interests and aims of the researchers
Message information value	Familiarize evaluators with the expertise level of the researcher
Usuability of Feedback	
Message validity	Give evaluators adequate information about research goals and the theoretical and methodological concerns of the researcher
Message specificity	Advise evaluators to avoid generalizations and to make their comments directly applicable to the work being reviewed
Message consistency	Give evaluators information on the evaluations done at earlier stages of the work; evaluators should provide reasons for their different appraisals
Message timeliness	Rather than follow a present schedule, arrange evaluation at the critical stages of the work; have evaluators who are accessible to the researchers

(*Table 9-2. continued overleaf*)

Table 9-2. continued

Criteria for Effective Feedback	Suggested Institutional Measures
Outcomes of Feedback	
Instrumental: direction	Evaluators should comment on deviations from the research goals and on what steps are required to get the research back on track
Instrumental: motivation	Evaluators should point out both strengths and weaknesses of the work, as well as encourage the researcher; on the annual performance review, institutions should as a matter of course reward dedication and extra effort
Instrumental: growth	Evaluators should descriptively point out the contributions of the researcher and offer encouragement; institutions should support research efforts with time and resources
Instrumental: attitude shaping	Institution should commit its resources not only to short-term but to long-term projects, thus enabling researchers to make major commitments to certain research areas
Performance: output	Imaginative and flexible allocation of material and human resources at the institutional level

Source: Mary Ann Von Glinow and Nirmal Sethia, in *Producing Useful Knowledge for Organizations*, edited by Kilmann, et al. (copyright © 1983 by Praeger Publishers, New York). Reprinted with permission.

a result of a study of 136 high-technology and professional employees from several departments of a large oil company located on the East Coast, as reported in Von Glinow and Sethia (1983).

Feedback Acceptance

To enhance the chances of acceptance, it is clear that knowledgeable and trustworthy colleagues who have the ability to link the performance feedback with subsequent rewards should deliver the feedback to the professional. We know that professionals demand autonomy; therefore, measures designed to allow them to pursue a particular type of research should be implemented, without reprisals. Further, career growth requires that they have the freedom to experiment, retool, and change, and that they have periodic time-outs, when traditional performance criteria are not enforced. Finally, a firm may wish to enlighten the evaluators by giving them detailed information about the professional, the project aims, and the like (Von Glinow and Sethia 1983).

Feedback Usability

The extent to which a firm can increase the usability of the feedback for the professional is contingent upon giving the evaluators appropriate information about the professional's expected performance and actual performance. Sometimes that means that evaluations should be given at critical junctures in the professional's work rather than at prescheduled times, which is common for most firms. Being able to give specific feedback is critical at this stage. In general, the more specific the feedback is, the better it is.

Feedback Outcomes

Finally, the outcomes of the feedback should be monitored. To do this, a firm must emphasize the importance of short-term as well as long-term project success, both of which can be achieved if a firm is flexible in its allocation of material and human resources. In addition to maintaining such flexibility, other measures might include systematically directing the goals of the research team, or encouraging the professionals by supporting their efforts with time and money.

It should also be mentioned that performance feedback may derive not only from the evaluators but from the task itself. The successful completion of some tasks imparts information about whether performance was excellent or not.

Too often a firm assumes that the outcome of the feedback is the most important aspect of the appraisal process. This chapter sought to explain that problems may arise much earlier in the PA process, problems such as the professional not accepting the feedback as credible, or not being able to use the feedback. Such factors significantly influence whether the PA will be successful or not and should routinely be considered in the appraisal process (Von Glinow forthcoming).

10 ORGANIZATIONAL STRUCTURES TO ACCOMMODATE PROFESSIONAL CAREER DEVELOPMENT

The provision of career growth and development is simultaneously an important reward for most high-technology and professional workers and one of the biggest sources of conflict for them. The nature of technical and professional work is such that continuing technical education and career development is essential. There also seem to be few role models for career engineers (Bailyn 1982); this lack exacerbates the potential for conflict for those professionals.

The key dilemma for technical and professional workers is whether to follow one's technical bent into isolation, with little chance of recognition, or to aspire to management, however untalented for it. Technical specialists will probably find it difficult to get the psychic income they need from managerial roles (Miller 1986; Bailyn 1982; Drucker 1988). That career route is not only more typical, but has much more cachet in this society.

There is an abundance of writing in the late 1980s about careers, by researchers and practitioners alike. Much of the attention is on the managerial career because it proceeds through various stages analogous to life stages. Comparatively little attention is paid to technical careers, despite the projections of acute shortages in technical and professional expertise in the years ahead. Two of the few studies that do exist on career professionals within high-tech industries reveal that engineers still working as engineers had much more negative

137

reactions to their work than did other engineers who had moved into management (Bailyn 1982; Bailyn and Lynch 1983). Career engineers were less satisfied with their work and tended to see themselves as less successful, despite the fact that many of them were prized by their employing organizations. But those with managerial assignmentments are valued more highly than those without such assignments. Having a successful career in engineering usually means leaving it. Hughes (1958) said it best, thirty years ago: "The engineer who, at forty, can still use a slide rule or logarithmic table, and make a true drawing, is a failure" (p. 137).

Of course, there have been many attempts to offer parallel opportunities to professionals who choose to stay in their technical specialty rather than take managerial posts. But generally, these dual ladders have met with failure. Technical professionals have largely rejected them as well, in part because the reward structures are heavily biased toward management positions and titles (Drucker 1988). Given historical and current organizational realities, career development for technical professionals appears to be a contradiction in terms. That is, the type of work that challenges the technical professional is not consistent with the organizationally defined "successful" career path for these employees (Bailyn 1982). Thus, the dilemma as well as the challenge to management rests in resolving this contradiction.

CONSTRAINTS ON THE HIGH-TECH FIRM THAT AFFECT ACCOMMODATION

Environmental Context

Adjusting to changes in competitive environments characterized by explosive growth, rapid technological change, and problems with employment practices, economic downturns, and reduced federal support for research, requires that firms be able to adapt their strategy quickly to be effective in their markets. They are frequently called upon to make adjustments in procedures, in work relationships among professionals, and in their organizational structures (Schoonhoven and Eisenhardt 1987). As a result of environmentally induced changes, many firms are forced to change their internal structures and emphases to speed up the cycle from research to development to production. In some cases, the link between research and production must be strengthened, and the link between development and manufacturing tightened (Bailyn 1982; Schoonhoven and Eisenhardt 1987).

These changes can profoundly affect what the high-tech firm considers its criteria for success, how important stakeholders are to its mission, and the time frame for its work. As a high-tech firm goes from start-up through its evolutionary stages, it has the potential to increase its revenues to hundreds of millions of dollars and to expand its work force from a handful of people to thousands, in a period of five years (Bahrami and Evans 1987). This development requires some type of quick transition from an entrepreneurial start-up to a large, complex enterprise. Of course, many fledgling firms never survive either the liability of newness (Stinchcombe 1965)—because of which young organizations are particularly prone to failure—or the anatomy of the "living dead" (Bourgeois and Eisenhardt 1987), which describes those firms not sufficiently successful to be taken public, but not clearly failing enough to die.

Since the most fundamental currency of exchange in high-technology industries is knowledge—which resides in the professional and high-technology workers—spin-offs from established firms and the shifting of key people between firms can alter industry dynamics substantially (Bahrami and Evans 1987). Spin-offs in high-tech firms located in technopolii benefit from a large pool of experts, opportunities associated with growing markets, and the possibility of lucrative rewards from holding equity in these start-up firms (Bahrami and Evans 1987). The external environment associated with firms operating in technopolii provides not only a "laboratory" for quickly testing ideas but also a supply of venture capital that allows good ideas to become funded.

Thus, environmental conditions are bound to influence the work relationships, the procedures for career advancement, and the structures of these high-tech firms. Bailyn (1982) notes that as a firm responds to environmental changes—response being critical at the firm level—a series of four internal contradictions arise that interfere with the degree of career and work satisfaction of technical professionals. She maintains that these contradictions are not the result of ill will, but stem from the complexities of growth, development, and change. They do tend, however, to frustrate the professionals and high-technology workers to the point where they opt out of the employment contract. These contradictions have their roots in the characteristics of professional workers and are identified below (Bailyn 1982).

Organizationally Induced Contradictions

Autonomy Versus Control.   As discussed in Chapter 3, high-technology and professional workers aspire to operational autonomy and resist managerial attempts at control. Just as there are professionals who fit that mold, however, there are others who do not. There is evidence to suggest that the scientists demand strategic autonomy, whereas the engineers wish to retain control over day-to-day decisions. Hence, a firm must take into consideration that, for example, engineering professionals and successful engineering careers come in many different forms (Bailyn and Lynch 1983). Managers who wish to accommodate the career aspirations of their professional and high-tech work force must present choices of career growth opportunities (Miller 1986). For example, professionals who do not fit the stereotype of the scholar-scientist and who want to be given projects that are central to the firm's mission, with operational autonomy to work on those projects, do not need autonomy in choosing an assignment.

The key is in recognition. If the organizational reward system is accurately recognizing differences in personnel, then ideally there will be organizational forms and practices that reflect those differences (Bailyn 1982; Bailyn and Lynch 1983; Bailyn 1985).

Stability Versus "Shake the Box."   A common response to environmental pressures is to reorganize the firm, or "shake the box" periodically. Some high-tech firms regularly shake the box to get rid of complacency and stagnation. Others do so because of high uncertainty levels. The evidence to date is that in many research labs and high-tech firms, such reorganizations entail tremendous cost (Hannan and Freeman 1984). Professionals see little reason for many so-called reorganizations, particularly when project stability is threatened. From the organization's point of view, however, combining functions and centralizing procedures may make sense. But change for the sake of change makes very little sense. The key is in communicating and justifying the need for such changes, particularly as they impact the professional's work and career concerns.

Linear Versus Lateral Career Crises. Most workers in the United States aspire to promotion. Driver (forthcoming) refers to these workers as "linears"; they define career success solely in terms of upward mobility. Many professionals and high-technology workers are linears. Given the nature of most pyramid-shaped organizations, however, most employees are stymied in their quest for upward mobility after a certain point.

This reality includes the high-tech work force. Alternate career concepts exist, but little is done organizationally to accommodate the career aspirations of the many workers who prefer to work in their specialty areas, who do not aspire to upward linear movement. The key is in recognizing different career concepts and in organizationally accommodating these differences through lateral promotions, transfers, or other methods. Most firms maintain that they want to accommodate their high-tech work force through attention to career needs. But most firms rarely investigate alternative structures for accommodating different career types.

Career Versus Work. A fourth contradiction arises when professionals position themselves so as to enhance their careers, but that positioning conflicts with the work itself. Bailyn (1982) notes that career advancement typically involves being visible to management, while effective work is often not visible to management. As with the other internal contradictions, some professionals will be career-oriented while others will be work-minded. Bailyn (1982) maintains that each type requires a different resolution. The professionals primarily interested in their technical work need alternative forms of recognition to keep them effective. These can come in the shape of different professional or career rewards, which may include placement on the dual ladder.

For those professionals and high-tech workers who aspire to hierarchical advancement, another dilemma occurs. If promotions occur too rapidly at the beginning of a professional's career, he or she runs the risk of future stagnation. Bailyn (1982) suggests that it might be better to slow down the promotions of younger professionals, while accelerating those of older career professionals. This is a reversal of the usual pattern. Workers who are somewhat ambivalent about their technical jobs—particularly the younger ones—should be encouraged to "try out" management, without making a long-term commitment or having important rewards withheld. Temporary assignments have had some success as a career reward for professionals.

ORGANIZATIONAL SOLUTIONS

Managing a high-technology and professional work force involves recognition of the fact that contradictions exist. Most perspectives seem to differ on steps toward resolution of those contradictions. Four structural accommodations have been discussed regularly in the literature and are listed below. Each of these structural solutions has empirical support, but each has also experienced controversial implementation. Miller (1986) and others have reminded us that the primary solution is to present the professional with a choice of career growth opportunities, so that he or she does not have to aspire to management. Dual ladders, triple hierarchies, temporary assignments, and a variety of career management programs have been implemented with varying degrees of success. The following section examines the most popular solutions to accommodating the career concerns of professionals.

Dual Ladders

In an attempt to mitigate the professional-organizational conflict and to provide professionals with alternative career paths, some firms have implemented a dual-ladder structure. The dual ladder is a set of positions for professionals that is designed to be parallel to the managerial ladder, but with evaluation, control, authority, and advancement criteria appropriate for the technical professional. The objectives of using such a dual ladder are: to provide advancement opportunities for professionals who are unable or unwilling to ascend the managerial ladder; to provide compensation, recognition, and prestige equivalent to that of successful managers; to provide professionals with greater autonomy; and to create a set of positions with administrative duties light enough to not interfere with professional contributions (Hallenberg 1970; Healey 1960; Kornhauser 1962; Secrist 1960; Miller 1986; Raelin 1987; Schriesheim, Von Glinow, and Kerr 1977). Figure 10-1 illustrates the single- and dual-ladder hierarchy structures.

Figure 10–1. Single and Dual Hierarchies.

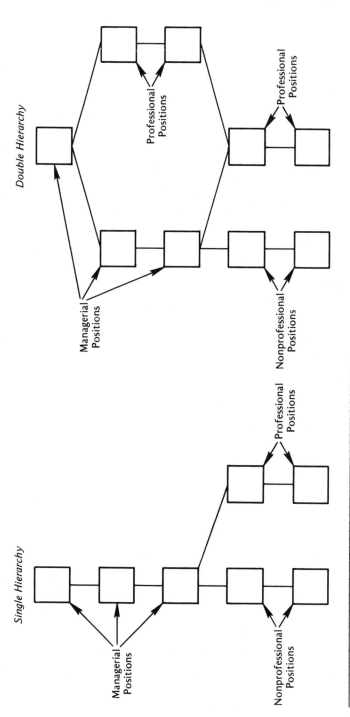

Source: Janet Schriesheim, Mary Ann Von Glinow, and Steven Kerr, "Professionals in Bureaucracies: A Structural Alternative," in *Prescriptive Models of Organizations*, ed. Paul Nystrom and William Starbuck, North-Holland TIMS Studies in the Management Sciences, vol. 5 (Amsterdam: North-Holland, 1977), pp. 55–69.

The success of the dual ladder is mixed (Raelin 1987; Miller 1986). In reviewing dual-ladder programs in which professionals may choose either a technical or a managerial ladder, and both ladders carry the same prestige, salary, and responsibility, Raelin (1987) found that the concept is a viable one. He noted that pitfalls stem from improper operation rather than from distorted logic.

Miller (1986) notes that even the best dual-ladder programs receive about equal numbers of complaints from nonmanagerial professionals as from managers. Problems around the perception of unfair promotions predominate. Managers who are seen as managerial failures, but who are transferred and subsequently promoted on the technical ladder, can generate the sentiment that the technical ladder is a dumping ground for unsuccessful managers (Miller 1986).

It is very difficult to make both sides of the ladder really equivalent, although there are many reported successes. Westinghouse, IBM, and Goodyear, to name but a few, have claimed success with their dual ladders. Sacco and Knopka (1983) report that six criteria must be met for the dual ladder to be successful. The program must (1) have senior management support and commitment; (2) have credibility with employees; (3) be flexible and adapt to change; (4) define the levels of technical contribution at each rung in the ladder; (5) have a review process to assure quality; and (6) have a high profile, through publicity both inside and outside the firm.

Riggs (1983) maintains that equity in pay is not enough to ensure success; dual ladders must involve recognition as well as compensation with recognition being by far the more difficult to implement.

Triple Hierarchies

A variation on the dual ladder, the "triple hierarchy," provides three different advancement opportunities. The managerial hierarchy is available to those who want promotions into managerial positions. The dual ladder or technical ladder is available to those who want only professional and technical positions. The third ladder, called a "liaison hierarchy," is occupied by professionals in key administrative positions. They have regular technical duties, but also have hierarchical authority over professionals in those areas where professional characteristics and organizational goals are most apt to conflict (Schriesheim, Von Glinow, and Kerr 1977). Figure 10–2 illustrates a

Figure 10-2. Triple Hierarchy.

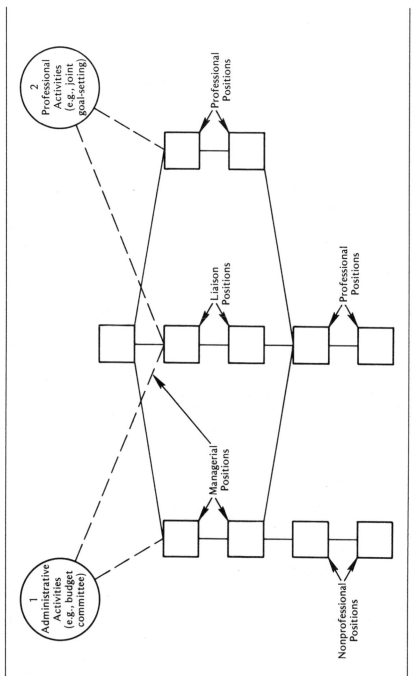

Source: Janet Schriesheim, Mary Ann Von Glinow, and Steven Kerr, "Professionals in Bureaucracies: A Structural Alternative," in *Prescriptive Models of Organizations*, ed. Paul Nystrom and William Starbuck, North-Holland TIMS Studies in the Management Sciences, vol. 5 (Amsterdam: North-Holland, 1977), pp. 55-69.

Table 10-1. Comparable Areas of Managerial and Liaison Authority.

Managerial Hierarchy	Liaison Hierarchy
Purchasing of general clerical supplies and equipment	Purchasing of specialized technical supplies and equipment
Selection and training of office and low-level administrative personnel	Selection and training of professional and technical personnel
Supervision of nonprofessional managerial and office personnel	Supervision and coordination of professional activities
Responsibility for evaluation of office and low-level administrative personnel	Responsibility for conducting or coordinating professional employee performance appraisals
Distribution of resources required by nonprofessional employees	Distribution of resources required by professional employees
Budgeting for nonprofessional activities	Budgeting for professional activities

triple hierarchy, with the managerial and technical ladders in place as well.

In those areas with high potential for conflict, managers have no authority. Such areas tend to vary by organization. Table 10-1 briefly describes some areas where the liaison hierarchy would take precedence over the managerial hierarchy in most organizations.

In essence, "liaisons" represent the interests of both managerial and professional subgroups. They should be involved in processes such as controling resources and planning functions, thus acquiring knowledge of the organizational constraints on resource allocation that affect the professionals. Similarly, liaisons can represent professionals on matters of company policy goal-setting, and resource allocation. This third ladder is, in effect, the buffer between the managerial and technical ladders.

Triple hierarchies have several advantages over dual-ladder systems. The most frequently stated reason for the failure of dual ladders is that professionals must rely on nonprofessionals for resources and services. The strength of the triple hierarchy is that it limits managerial authority to allocating resources and services to nonprofessionals only. Liaisons allocate resources and services to professionals, thus buffering both sides from one another.

Another advantage of the triple hierarchy over the dual ladder is that the triple hierarchy is more likely to equitably evaluate professionals, since evaluations and recommendations for promotion of professionals are made by liaisons, not by managers (Schriesheim, Von Glinow, and Kerr 1977).

A final problem—which is neither enhanced nor diminished by the triple hierarchy structural arrangement—is the continued perception of inequity across ladders, the perception that placement on the professional ladder is evidence of failure, or of an inadequate number of professional positions. This problem may emerge under the triple hierarchy, just as it does under the dual-ladder system; however, the triple hierarchy would not necessarily bring this problem about.

Temporary Assignments

As previously mentioned, temporary assignments can play an important role in an organization employing high-technology and professional employees. These assignments may be to management or other kinds of tasks, to different phases of the R&D process—for example, from research to development—or to groups using different technologies (Bailyn 1982). These temporary or new assignments can alleviate stagnation, give recognition, and allow professionals to reapply their skills in different work situations. Bailyn (1982) notes that even the negative effects of constant reorganizations may be obviated when new organization charts are seen to apply more to jobs than to the people doing the jobs.

There are, of course, inherent problems in managing within a fluid, flexible environment that utilizes temporary assignments. There are costs associated with start-up for each job change, or each temporary assignment, as well as the possibility, as Bailyn (1982) says, that the reassigned person may not be able to handle the new job. These costs are reflected in the firm's tracking system. How is performance determined for professionals on temporary assignment? How are rewards allocated? Who is ultimately responsible for these people?

When temporary assignments are performed at home on the computer, additional problems of control emerge (Metzger and Von Glinow forthcoming). The use of temporary assignments is not meant as a panacea; however, they are generally useful in the short term to alleviate specific problems.

Career Development Support

Career development has typically been the domain of the first-line supervisor (Walker and Gutteridge 1979) and has rarely been done well, particularly for professional and high-tech workers. Miller (1986) notes that career development support begins with training professionals and managers in the importance of the process of career management, which begins with improving the person-job fit. He claims that truly progressive high-tech firms begin career development programs as a part of the larger effort to improve productivity and reduce turnover.

Support for career development must be done within the prevailing culture of the firm. Thus, caring culture firms will likely support career development differently from exacting culture firms. Nevertheless, it seems that three types of support are fundamental to this process: top-management support; support for training of both managers and professionals in the methods of career management; and support through a firm's policies and procedures, which should allow the manager to sit down with the professional at least once a year for a career discussion.

Top-management support is not particularly controversial. The latter two—the training of managers and professionals in the methods, or "how-to" of managing their careers, and the career-thinking focus of a firm's policies and procedures—are somewhat controversial. For the past twenty years, U.S. firms have become much more attentive to career concerns (Dowd and Sonnenfeld 1984). This concern is manifested in a variety of career development activities. Some firms have formal career management programs; others try to incorporate some type of career-thinking into the annual performance appraisal. Most of these efforts fall into one of eight broad categories (Arnold and Feldman 1986; Morgan, Hall, and Martier 1979; Feldman 1988). The following are some of the more commonly practiced career management programs for professionals and high-tech workers (Feldman 1988).

Career Information Systems. Many firms, including 3M and Lawrence Livermore Lab, actively disseminate information in-house about career opportunities. Jobs are posted, and professionals may nominate themselves for new positions. In some cases, information about career paths into key jobs is also provided.

Human-Resource Planning and Forecasting. Some firms—Rockwell International and Hewlett-Packard, among them—have computerized skills inventories of their workers. When new positions open up, the firm has a list of all the employees whose repertoire of skills fits the position description. Feldman (1988) notes that many firms now require their workers to prepare job replacement charts. Supervisors must document what training each of their subordinates would need for promotion, and their plans for providing that training (Hall 1976).

Career Counseling. Career counselors may be from the HR department or from outside professional services, or they may be professionals trained in the technical specialty of the individual requesting career counseling. In other words, this option covers a broad array of services. In-house career counseling programs have increased dramatically within the last decade. Most career counseling begins with some type of self-assessment and with exercises designed to identify the important steps the employee must take to achieve his or her goals. At Lawrence Livermore Lab, technical and scientific professionals who hold graduate degrees in counseling psychology are employed as career counselors (Miller 1978).

Career Sequencing and Monitoring. As an alternative to random job placement, many organizations are beginning to sequence and monitor jobs for their high-tech work forces. In this way, career movements have a logic attached to them. In many high-tech firms, or in firms employing a great number of high-technology and professional workers, the dual ladder structurally serves this purpose. The burden is frequently placed on the manager, however, to ascertain strengths and weaknesses and to calibrate those on a reasonable career path for each employee.

Skills Assessment and Training. This type of career management program has its roots in the methodologies of the "assessment centers," pioneered by AT&T many years ago. This type of program is generally for mid to late career employees, whose skills may need bolstering in some specific areas. To supplement this type of training, some in-house technical training of professionals may be utilized. Most companies today, in fact, offer some type of in-house training program to upgrade either technical or managerial skills. Tuition reimbursements are offered to many technical specialists, and to others seeking to upgrade their credentials, along with release time to pursue advanced degrees at local universities. The alternative concept of the "corporate college," however, is becoming more and more popular.

Career Development for Disadvantaged Groups. Many firms are seeking ways of helping employees who, historically, have been discriminated against in the United States. Enhanced recruitment and selection efforts, along with monitoring career movement for these minority employees, have become commonplace. Some firms even run career management seminars designed specifically for women, minorities, and late entrants into the work force (Morgan, Hall, and Martier 1979).

Career Development for Fast-Track Employees. For high-tech and professional employees who have the "right stuff," most firms are more apt to exert extra recruitment efforts and may monitor career progress as often as every six months. These valued employees receive counseling and training on an as-needed basis. Managers seem to be particularly sensitive to providing high potential workers with especially challenging work assignments.

Career Development Workshops for Supervisors. In most firms, the first-line supervisor is responsible for career development. Many firms are now expending considerable effort on training these supervisors in counseling, coaching, and career counseling. AT&T, for example, trains supervisors in job restructuring, joint goal-setting, career counseling, and performance appraisal skill development (Miller 1978).

Integrated Career-Thinking

It seems clear from the evidence so far that firms with successful career management programs for their high-tech and professional work force have integrated career development into their human-resource systems (Von Glinow, Driver, Brousseau, and Prince 1983; Feldman 1988). Further, these firms make good use of career rewards, which may even be based on length of service. Immediate-line supervisors are highly involved in career management techniques. Typically, there are periodic skills assessments, and these occur throughout the career of the professional.

Implicit in this process, of course, is realistic, credible feedback, given by someone trustworthy. Equally important is top-management support for these activities. It has been frequently documented that the most successful career development programs focus on job assignments and job design (Miller 1986) rather than on career advancement (Feldman 1988). Advancement is a promise that many firms simply cannot deliver; therefore, it is best to concentrate on career development for current job success. The concept of temporary assignments allows flexibility in job assignments and reward systems. As was previously discussed, different types of rewards can be linked to different factors, including age, skill level, and the like.

In summary, there are a variety of structures that can accommodate a professional's career growth and development. When we consider that career growth routinely emerges as an important source of loyalty to the organization as well as an important reward, the structures that can enhance a professional's career development should be seriously considered. At a time when the high-tech revolution has deeply affected almost all industries, career development must be central.

11 MANAGING CHANGE AND GROWTH OF INTERNATIONAL COMPETITION

Throughout this book, we have seen that high-tech firms are characterized by rapid innovations, inventions, short product life cycles, rapid new product developments, employment of many high-tech and professional employees, and tremendous domestic as well as international competition. In short, they are characterized by a tremendous amount of change.

Companies are spending literally billions of dollars each year to research and develop new products (Rogers 1981). Firms that operate in high-technology environments, or are affiliated with a technopolis, must be able to adapt their strategies quickly to be effective participants in their markets. Further, they are frequently required to make changes to their work force, their organizational structures, and their procedures (Schoonhoven 1986). The rate and pace of change is phenomenal. Some industries derive most of their current business from products that did not exist five years ago. Such technological change worries a lot of companies, and they are "scrambling even harder to anticipate the accelerating twists and turns" (Duke 1987: 33D).

Some firms, like National Cash Register and Minnesota Mining and Manufacturing, are dealing with the continuing impact of technological change by streamlining internal research, by changing their previously unwieldy bureaucratic structures to more nimble independent units, and by joining research consortia to share the risks of changes in technology (Duke 1987). Some are going so far as to develop technology strategies that are integrated with their business strategies (Hamilton 1985; Friar and Horwitch 1985; Mitchell 1985).

With all of this comes the recognition that technological change is a prerequisite to economic growth (Roman 1980) and organizational effectiveness for high-tech firms. This chapter takes a critical look at the impact of technological change on organizational structures and at how best to manage in view of this change. It also describes how international competition is accelerating the rate and pace of change for high-tech firms.

THE IMPACT OF TECHNOLOGICAL CHANGE ON ORGANIZATIONAL STRUCTURES

Since technologies, markets, and competitive boundaries are in a state of constant change, high-tech firms are faced with fairly unique organizational challenges (Bahrami and Evans 1987). They need to quickly respond to new developments and opportunities by adapting their structures and processes to fit technological and environmental conditions (Schoonhoven and Eisenhardt 1987; Galbraith 1977; Chandler 1962; Lawrence and Lorsch 1969). In addition, managers in the firms no longer have the luxury of planning years in advance, on the assumption that the rules will be the same in the years ahead (Duke 1987). According to Bahrami and Evans (1987), high-tech firms must be flexible, able to accommodate impermanent tasks, be organized for focused action, and must retain the spirit of entrepreneurialism as well as their innovative capability.

Historically, bureaucracies have been quite useful organizational structures in stable environments. When the environment becomes volatile, however, as in the case of most high-tech firms today, bureaucratic structures do not give management sufficient leeway to address the imperatives confronting the firm. The classic work of Burns and Stalker (1961), followed by structural contingency theory (Lawrence and Lorsch 1967; Galbraith 1977), argued that more organic structures were appropriate for uncertain technological and environmental circumstances. This thinking has prevailed in the management literature for decades now; however, it has recently been challenged by those scholars focusing on the structural impact of technological changes (Schoonhoven and Eisenhardt 1987; Bourgeois and Eisenhardt 1987). They argue that the usual prescription of organic structures falls short of its promises and fails to deal with the "liability of newness" problems associated with most young high-tech firms.

According to the "liability of newness" arguments, young organizations are particularly prone to failure (Schoonhoven and Eisenhardt 1987). Van de Ven, Hudson, and Schroeder (1984) reported that 46 percent of all new firms in the United States fail within eighteen months of their founding. Hannan and Freeman (1984) argue that young firms have a tendency to change, and that these changes have a negative impact on performance. Further, those changes "reset the 'liability of newness' clock by scrambling the relationships and roles within the organization" (Schoonhoven and Eisenhardt 1987: 7). Therefore, they claim, the best performing young firms are those that "quickly develop clear, reproducible structures and gain structural inertia" (p. 7).

Schoonhoven and Eisenhardt (1987) go on to argue that the problem with organic structures for high-tech firms is that they fail to deal with "twin tensions." On the one hand, the uncertainty of technological change requires organizational flexibility; on the other hand, continuity and control are mandatory for the process of new product development and manufacturing.

Thus, the most current thinking on organizational structures in rapidly changing environments maintains that clear, stable organizational structures are the most appropriate. These structures maintain their adaptability through frequent reorganizations, the use of temporary teams, and rational planning systems (Schoonhoven and Eisenhardt 1987; Bailyn 1982), thus fulfilling the requirement of flexibility. This current thinking concludes that both bureaucratic and organic structures are inappropriate for high-tech firms facing rapidly changing technological environments.

Structural Characteristics of High-Tech Firms

The organizational mandate is to design structures that are fluid and flexible, while maintaining cohesion across interdependent functional and technological activities (Bahrami and Evans 1987). While many different structures exist for high-tech firms, the following characteristics have become standard among most of them (Bahrami and Evans 1987; Schoonhoven and Eisenhardt 1987).

Frequent Reorganizations.   The stated rationale for frequent reorganizations is to allow the "clear design" organizations to readily adapt to internal and external demands. Organizations that have clear, formalized structures, which are either known by managers and employees alike or are formalized through organizational charts are referred to as "clear design" organizations. Since high-tech firms are frequently in the midst of product and process changes as well as competitive uncertainty, clear structure provides an element of predictability for employees and organizational units alike (Schoonhoven and Eisenhardt 1987). Responsibilities change during frequent reorganizations, and this is appropriate in view of external and technological changes facing the firm (Schoonhoven and Eisenhardt 1987). Successful new firms have been found to adapt through frequent reorganizations rather than through the use of organic structures with ambiguous job descriptions and reporting relationships. These reorganizations may be abrupt, however, with little notice or forethought on the part of the firm (Schoonhoven and Eisenhardt 1987).

As mentioned in Chapter 10, these reorganizations have their costs. Since new roles must be established, and new relationships created, the firm periodically experiences the same chaos that is typical of organic structures (Hannan and Freeman 1984).

Multiple Roles, Temporary Teams, and Temporary Assignments.
Individuals in high-tech firms generally have multiple roles and are rotated through a variety of assignments, depending on the firm's priorities (Bahrami and Evans 1987). Rotation can stretch the employee tremendously, but serves other goals as well. It broadens an individual's skill base, thus fostering career growth. Similarly, rotation provides a firm with some leeway in dealing with new challenges as they arise. Multiple roles are designed to "leverage the capabilities of individuals, rather than to fulfill predetermined roles through stable positions in the hierarchy" (Bahrami and Evans 1987: 54). Temporary teams and assignments also add a cushion of flexibility between subunits of the firm's formal structure.

Project Teams and Task Forces.   Since most high-tech firms are engaged in knowledge and information acquisition, transfer, and dissemination, project teams and special task forces can bring together different blends of expertise for different activities. For example, synthetic fibers resulted from a combination of efforts in the textile and chemical industries (Hamilton 1985). Complementary activities are frequently represented in the founding team of many start-up ventures; that mix is a major criterion of venture capitalists assessing the potential of the new venture.

It is interesting that task forces generally are disbanded after they have completed their mission. However brief their duration, task forces have been known to have a strong impact on their members. Indirectly, they engender commitment from team members and may be used to champion new products as well as to implement decisions.

Coordination Via Frequent Communication. In view of the frequent reorganizations and the adjustments made to technology or business strategies, high-tech firms rely on continual communication for coordination purposes (Bahrami and Evans 1987). This attention to communication is underscored by the amount of time spent on informal meetings and one-on-one interactions. To some extent, even formal activities are used as communication opportunities. The emergence of E-mail and computerized voice-messaging systems also facilitates the flow of information and communication. Teleconferencing and video conferencing systems can now link multiple, diverse geographical areas. Bahrami and Evans (1987) remind us that, in addition to the formal communication networks, informal interactions such as company parties and the like are useful in enhancing communication flows.

The Staff Function. The role of the staff is minimized within most high-tech firms, since coordination is achieved through communication rather than by standardized processes, outputs, and skills (Bahrami and Evans 1987). In addition, high-tech firms within a technopolis can avail themselves of an intricate external environment, thus avoiding the high costs associated with internal staff departments. Many high-tech firms, such as Xerox, have downsized their staff functions in favor of hiring external consultants on an as-needed basis.

As in most firms, the line makes the decisions, and staff is expected to support the line operation. Since many high-tech firms are less pyramidal-shaped, they have fewer layers of staff. Many companies rotate line personnel through the existing staff functions—again, on temporary assignment. Deemphasized staff functions also tend to foster greater interaction between line functions.

Hierarchical Configurations.   Most high-tech firms have an organizational structure that resembles a matrix (Kanter 1984), which allows them to respond quickly to technological change. The matrix design has the high-tech or professional worker and the manager reporting in basically two directions, in an attempt to decentralize decision-making while maintaining centralized control (Kanter 1984). The matrix design grew out of the postwar aerospace industry, where large programs were carried out by teams from a number of different functional units. Under matrix conditions, reporting and performance appraisal become much more complex; however, different types of expertise are more easily brought to projects.

To the matrix, Bahrami and Evans (1987) add that the operating core of the firm is firmly integrated with the "apex" of the firm as represented by the senior management team. They note that this structure differs from traditional, pyramidal-shaped forms in two important ways. First, the staff and line are well integrated in traditional firms, whereas high-tech firms have a line hierarchy exclusively. Second, power is exercised in high-tech firms through influence, not through authority per se. Taylor (1986) maintains that the same people are consistently seen as influential gatekeepers, regardless of changes in the firm's structure. Thus, expertise is the mainstay of the high-tech firm and is exercised through influence (Bahrami and Evans 1987).

Grouping of Functions.   Bahrami and Evans (1987) note that because of short product life cycles, high-tech firms tend to diversify into related businesses relatively early. Thus, innovative environments are maintained through smaller units. This is quite common; having many smaller units tends to retain the entrepreneurial spirit. The key is in ensuring that the various small units within the firm remain integrated. Bahrami and Evans (1987) maintain that this necessity gives rise to hybrid organizations. For example, one type of hybrid might be the coupling of a divisional substructure with a functional or geographical superstructure. When we remember that constant reorganization is also the norm within high-tech firms, it becomes apparent that such groupings of activities or units may change in response to changes in technology or business strategy.

Control Systems. Generally speaking, high-tech firms do not maintain control by standardized rules and procedures. There is considerable change associated with most jobs; thus, we see little of the operating procedures typical of the large, bureaucratic firms. Instead, each firm develops its own control system, which is likely to vary depending upon the type of culture the firm maintains. If the firm is highly performance-driven, then output controls predominate and emphasis is placed on meeting objectives. In the many high-tech firms whose professionals have an equity position in the firm, employees becoming owners serves as an additional means of control (Bahrami and Evans 1987).

Planning Systems and Decisionmaking. There is evidence now that planning plays a very important role in high-tech firms (Schoonhoven and Eisenhardt 1987). Particularly in the early stages of the life of the new firm, planning is critical to anticipating problems such as a slowdown of cash flow or a short delay in product introduction. The more closely the entrepreneurs follow a planning model made before the founding of the firm, the stronger the organizational performance after start-up is (Van de Ven 1980).

Decisionmaking tends to be decentralized in high-tech firms, since line personnel usually have a say in the firm's strategy. But senior management is aware of all the key decisions, so that, in a sense, decisionmaking at these firms is simultaneously centralized and decentralized (Bahrami and Evans 1987).

Reward Systems. As we have seen in Chapters 5 and 6, rewards play a different role in high-tech firms than they do in more traditional manufacturing firms. It is not uncommon to find many employees with equity positions in the firm, through stock ownership. Additionally, we see a number of different types of rewards: for example, professional and career rewards, which have more currency than other incentives for attracting, motivating, and retaining high-tech and professional employees.

CHANGES THAT INCREASE A FIRM'S
CAPACITY TO MEET NEW CHALLENGES

The previous section described the typical structural components of the high-tech firm. Those structural components are changed in response to environmental shifts, crises, or other galvanizing events. Most successful high-tech firms, however, embrace a certain amount of change, unlike their large bureaucratic counterparts. Managing change is becoming more and more important because the rate and pace of change is increasing so dramatically. In view of the failure rate of new firms, the capacity to meet new challenges also becomes even more important.

Change not only results from forces internal and external to the high-tech firm, but it causes additional changes as well. The "change begets change" phenomenon is one reason why it is so difficult to develop a model of change for the high-tech firm. Unlike large, bureaucratic firms—where change typically occurs in a slow, incremental fashion (Kanter 1983)—high-tech firms live in the world of constant change. Whether a given change is "good" or "bad" depends on the outcome (Miller 1986). Even outcomes that seem "bad" in the short term may trigger events that will have a positive impact in the future. Thus, we will concentrate on changes that can help increase a firm's capacity to be fit for future action.

Firms change for five general reasons: (1) discomfort and departure from tradition; (2) to communicate a vision of desired goals; (3) crises and other startling events; (4) the strategic decisions of the leader; and (5) infrastructure capacity to accommodate change.

Discomfort and Departure from Tradition

Changes generally occur as a result of some type of discomfort. Miller (1986) suggests the term "hurt factor," which he likens to Lewin's (1951) "unfreezing-change-refreezing" model—a standard in the management textbooks since the 1960s. Discomfort may be the result of a random event, or it may be purposively brought about through the actions of people. Or it may result from some "black hole"—the indirect consequence of change from something unrelated (Kanter 1983).

Kanter (1983) maintains that discomfort arises from departures from the traditional way of doing things. In young high-tech firms, there may be very little tradition to fall back on. She maintains, however, that these departures from the established way of doing things are usually brought about by the "actions of entrepreneurs who seek to move beyond the job-as-given. They may be stimulated by a plan, in the form of an assignment, but they may also be invented by the entrepreneur . . . [who has] a problem to be solved" (Kanter 1983: 291). Miller (1986) claims that the subsequent challenge is to take the discomfort that the individual feels and transform it into motivation. In this way, departures from tradition contribute to an organization's memory by giving the individual or the firm a set of experiences that can be remembered when similar changes confront the firm in the future. The actions and methods that are used should therefore be loosely enough controlled that others are allowed the right to experiment (Kanter 1983). Success may lie within those new experiments. When a departure from tradition produces a positive outcome, this reinforces the firm's capacity to meet new challenges.

Communicating a Vision of Desired Goals

Most high-tech firms that successfully manage the changes that confront them have a founder, or a key leader, who has communicated his or her vision of the desired goals. Miller (1986) calls this the "dream factor"—visions, like dreams, can cause motivation. The vision helps to crystallize the overall view for all of the high-tech and professional workers (Drucker 1988). Once communicated, the vision becomes a standard against which the success of responses to subsequent changes are calibrated. If the vision has not been well articulated, the people who are involved in attaining the goals are not likely to "buy into it" as an important goal.

Visions, like dreams, can provide compensation during the pain of the change. Miller (1986) suggests that dreams make the pain worthwhile, and that they must be nurtured and maintained if they are to be useful in creating meaningful change.

Visions have concrete components, such as goals, which ideally are defined by the professionals who strive to accomplish them. If the high-tech and professional work force has participated in the process of defining those goals, it is more likely to feel ownership and pride in achieving those goals (Miller 1986). Visions, then, also create a capacity to meet future challenges.

Crises and Other Startling Events

Crises may be internal events—such as the introduction of new technologies that are not debugged—or external events—such as a new competitor entering the market. The important aspect of crises is that they require a response from the firm. Those responses generally entail making changes. Firms respond to crises, or impending crises, either reactively or proactively. Reactive firms tend to expend considerable energy on "fire fighting," whereas proactive firms anticipate the likelihood of crisis or unplanned events by planning for them. Such planning dovetails with the infrastructure capacity to accommodate change.

Nevertheless, crises tend to mandate swift and innovative responses from the high-tech firm. If the employees are capable of handling abrupt changes precipitated by a crisis, then others may be galvanized to search for innovative responses as well (Kanter 1983). We are reminded by Kanter (1983) that the effectiveness of a response to a given crisis may depend upon how capable the firm is of departing from its traditional response. If the firm is capable of responding in innovative ways and is not tied to a one best way of doing things, then it may not be too tradition-bound to meet these challenges.

The Strategic Decisions of the Leader

The role that the leader or the founder of the high-tech firm plays is critical in the change process. The leader generally holds the vision and stimulates the members' interest in change (Miller 1986). It is through his or her key strategic decisions that change is brought to fruition.

Since the strategic importance of technology is increasing, leaders are continually being faced with the need to make decisions about the technology to accomplish a wide range of strategic purposes (Mitchell 1985). These leaders are therefore likely to solicit input from a variety of individuals to help in framing the business or technology strategy. The strategic decisions are even more important when made within a crisis situation. When crises provoke radical changes—which often cause discontinuities in the evolution of products, processes, and markets—the ability to make thoughtful decisions is an important managerial challenge.

Leaders in high-tech firms make technology strategy decisions along three basic lines (Friar and Horwitch 1985: 151):

- competition versus cooperation (competitive strategy)

- internal versus external development (domain)

- traditional R&D organizations, e.g., the industrial R&D facility, versus decentralized entrepreneurial units (structure)

Judging the trade-offs between these choices is the primary task in the leader's strategic decisionmaking. His or her task is made easier if the firm has an infrastructure to help deal with these questions.

Infrastructure Capacity to Accommodate Change

Changes can be welcomed if a firm has mechanisms or infrastructures that allow the changes to be expressed. These infrastructures include a rational planning process, clear designs, and the ability to anticipate problems (Bourgeois and Eisenhardt 1987). A firm also needs an infrastructure that allows for flexibility in the institutionalization of changes. When institutionalizing change, a critical element is the ability to integrate the change with other parts of the system (Kanter 1983). If innovations or changes are pursued in isolation, it is unlikely that they will take hold in a productive fashion.

To fully integrate changes into a firm's business or technology strategy, it is important that other personnel and organizational functions be informed (Von Glinow, Driver, Brousseau, and Prince 1983). These functions must also be able to systematically integrate the new changes.

THE IMPACT OF INTERNATIONAL COMPETITION ON THE RATE OF CHANGE

There are many different social and economic factors that determine a nation's competitive advantage in world markets. Belous (1987) maintains that a country's wage rates are one of the most important determinants of how competitive a country will be internationally. He also notes, however, that low wage rates do not necessarily mean low unit labor costs.

Equally potent in determining international competitiveness is a country's foreign exchange rate. Knowledge of exchange rates, productivity, and unit labor costs could provide us with a useful picture of the U.S. competitive advantage in high tech. But Belous (1987) notes with dismay that we have little sound data on productivity or unit-labor cost estimates.

> Computers are a key part of the high tech sector, of course, yet the United States still does not have an official measure of U.S. computer industry productivity. . . . Thus, the United States faces stiff international competition without productivity and unit labor cost measures for many (if not most) central high tech products and industries (p. 42).

Madique and Hayes (1984) and Sexton (1988) note that the problem is exacerbated by the world's perception that management of high-tech firms in the United States has shifted from a position stronger than most in the late sixties and early seventies to marginally competent in the mid-eighties. The lack of concrete information on high-tech productivity, coupled with the perception that U.S. high tech is poorly managed, has led Birnbaum (1988) to the conclusion that the United States is doing very badly in its quest for world economic leadership in the 1990s. He notes that a number of prestigious commissions and professional associations have simultaneously reached the conclusion that the United States has lost national competitiveness in the last decades of the twentieth century.

The failure of American high-tech firms to keep pace with other countries (most notably with Japan and West Germany, but to some extent, with the newly industrialized countries of Korea, Taiwan, Singapore, and Hong Kong as well) in patents, invention rates, important innovations, and even suggestions from employees, has been attributed to poor management performance. In formulating business strategy, management has for many years emphasized marketing and short-term financial considerations (Riggs 1983). Such policies have not resulted in long-term success for the high-tech firms.

By way of contrast, most Japanese firms, as well as some of the better-run high-tech firms in the United States, take a long-term, less bottom-line–focused view of their businesses (Riggs 1983).

Most evidence now suggests that for firms to be internationally competitive, they must be willing to invest time and energy in the process of innovation and must seize the opportunities that new technologies afford (Rogers and Valente 1988; Riggs 1983).

Collaborative Efforts at Innovation

Cognizant of a steadily declining international position, many high-tech industries have shifted from encouraging a "dog-eat-dog" ethos to limited forms of collaboration on R&D activities, in an effort to offset the decline (Rogers and Larsen 1984). Principally located in the microelectronics industry, a number of consortia have been spawned over the last few years to share the risks of the high costs of innovation, as well as to beat the Japanese—the electronics industry's primary competitor.

One example of the shift from competition to collaboration within microelectronics is an R&D consortium called Microelectronics and Computer Technology Corporation (MCC), which was formed by twenty different companies wanting to collaborate on R&D activities (Rogers and Valente 1988). The consortium was intended to compete with the Fifth-Generation Computer Project, a Japanese consortium composed of MITI, Nippon Telephone and Telegraph Company, and the seven largest electronics companies in Japan. Rogers and Valente (1988) point out that the Fifth-Generation Computer Project was an outgrowth of Very Large Scale Integrated computers (VLSI), a similar Japanese consortium that produced "over a hundred patented innovations and which contributed to worldwide Japanese dominance in semiconductor memory chips" (p. 23).

Thus far, MCC is the most visible U.S. consortium. Each of those twenty firms has changed in response to international threats. In several cases, the firms have moved their R&D units close to MCC headquarters in Austin, Texas to avail themselves of the special environment of the MCC technopolis (Rogers and Valente 1988).

It is clear that international competition can and does affect the rate of change. While it is still too early to assess the magnitude or the success of that change, MCC for one seems to be following the trend established in the Silicon Valley of high-tech spin-offs (Rogers and Valente 1988).

It is likely that collaborative R&D ventures will increase in the future, in response to international competition. Change becomes a much less risky proposition if there are others to share the responsibility leading to technological innovations.

12 PUTTING IT ALL TOGETHER
Prescriptions for Success

There is no question that high-technology industries and the professional and high-tech work force are vital to the economic health and prosperity of the United States. The rapid development of high-tech industries and the subsequent demand for highly skilled scientists, engineers, and other technologically sophisticated specialists suggest that the third industrial revolution has now begun. The agents of change include the microprocessor, CAD/CAM, lasers, biogenetics, and a host of other new technologies (Finkelstein and Newman 1984).

At the core of these new technologies are the professionals and high-tech workers who research and develop the innovations that engineer change. This book has been concerned with the extent to which professional and high-tech workers are systematically different from nonprofessional workers. These differences demand innovative approaches to the management of human resources in high-tech industries. In turn, these innovative approaches to human-resource management are affected by the fact that high-tech firms operate within dynamic or "high velocity" environments (Bourgeois and Eisenhardt 1987). High tech is indeed transforming the way in which we live. It affects labor trends, employment patterns, the development of new products and markets, and global and domestic competition.

The central managerial challenge of the future is to design integrated systems that have a reflexive capability built into them. These systems must monitor and match the needs of the high-tech and pro-fessional workers with the goals of the firm. This is no easy challenge, since the goal of maximizing the productivity of high-tech and pro-fessional workers may be at variance with the values of these work-ers. This managerial challenge must also be played out within the context of unrelenting change.

In assessing key learnings about the management of these workers, it is useful to recap the nature of the high-tech work force, the man-agement of human resources, the management of the culture of the firm, and structural accommodations.

THE NATURE OF THE HIGH-TECH
WORK FORCE

There are several distinctive features of the high-tech and profes-sional work force. The workers are knowledge workers, and their expertise and talent are in substantial demand by most high-tech firms. These workers have value and attitudinal characteristics that vary significantly from those of other workers. They have invested heavily in their training and specialized knowledge, and they fre-quently have advanced degrees. They enjoy intellectual and technical challenges—or "puzzles," as Bailyn (1982) refers to them. Since they have expert training and skills, they tend to identify more with their profession or technology than with their employing organization. This can be a fundamental dilemma for the firm.

In addition, most high-tech and professional workers value and demand autonomy, and most good managers are aware of this. In fact, autonomy serves as a professional reward for many of these workers. They do not consider salary and fringe benefits as impor-tant as the meaningfulness of their work. Management must recog-nize this fact and reward these workers accordingly.

Other values include a strong sense of ethics and an internal per-formance standard that mitigates against traditional performance appraisal. Professionals identify more with others trained in their technical specialty. Nevertheless, these workers have a strategic im-portance to the firm that is becoming even more critical with increas-ing international competition.

High-tech and professional workers cluster in high-tech conglom-erations throughout the country, known as technopolii. These technopolii have brought significant changes to the labor markets they serve. Most technopolii have a strong affiliation with a research university, which they depend upon for talent.

Although Belous (1987) and other technological forecasters claim that there is not a general shortage of these high-tech and professional workers, there are indeed shortages in some skill areas that are needed for continued competitiveness. The U.S. government, through its attention to science and technology policy, seems aware of these shortages and committed to providing sufficient engineering and scientific talent to regain technological leadership (Kleingartner and Anderson 1987).

Other distinctive features of high tech are that the production processes are nonroutine, and knowledge is intensive (Gomez-Mejia and Balkin 1985). Many high-tech firms reinvest up to 20 percent of their revenues in R&D because they have a high obsolescence expectancy. Many high-tech firms are young and have been started by an entrepreneurial founder; they remain reasonably flexible in responding to environmental changes. Product life cycles tend to be fairly short and are measured more in terms of months than of years. In fact, most high-tech products have life cycles of approximately one to three years (Gomez-Mejia and Balkin 1985; Miljus and Smith 1987).

In view of the labor requirements for high-tech production, it is fair to say that "the industry tends to go where the costs are lowest . . . and has tended to expand where there has been a readily available pool of trained scientific and technical workers" (Kleingartner and Anderson 1987: 205).

All of these features of the high-tech work force have implications for the way in which a firm's human assets are managed.

THE MANAGEMENT OF HUMAN RESOURCES

There is an interesting, almost symbiotic, relationship between professional and high-tech workers and high-technology organizations. These firms have a large stake in developing innovative human-resource practices that thoughtfully attract, motivate, and retain these strategically important workers, and that maximize their productivity. Managers must recognize that a certain amount of tension, dissent, and conflict is natural, even when the firm has a well-articulated human-resource philosophy regarding these employees.

A pressing concern for human-resource professionals who must design systems to accommodate high-tech and professional workers is recruiting and training them. Due to the high cost of professional turnover, American industry has begun to put a tremendous amount of funds and energy into training and developmental programs for professionals. More and more, high-tech firms and HR system designers are encouraging professionals to continue their education, either through in-house training and degree-granting programs or through outside universities. HR professionals have recognized the importance of giving these workers "intellectual space," since creativity and innovation are difficult to mandate.

Designing reward systems that encourage the professional's talents is of primary concern. Much attention has been focused on financial incentives as the major means of attracting, motivating, and retaining these workers. Financial rewards have little salience for these workers, however, despite the repeated emphasis in the current literature on pay plans and exquisitely fashioned compensation options.

Instead, professional, career, and content rewards tend to be more valued by these workers. When managers pay attention to the unique characteristics and values of their professional workers, it is less difficult to understand that they are motivated and "driven" to perform by a whole different set of motivators. Critically important here is the challenge and meaningfulness of the work the professional performs. Equally important is that the work retain its meaningfulness over the course of the professional's career. Hence, paying attention to career development is a very important challenge for managers of these workers. Since career development historically has had no more impact than the "pet rock," the design of career-sensitive HR systems is one of the chief design problems of the high-tech firm.

Equally important to professional workers is the design of appropriate performance appraisal systems that are attentive to their standards of evaluation. Since professional workers are largely responsible for new product and process innovations, these employees become the gatekeepers of information. An important challenge for managers of these gatekeepers is to accurately assess performance within the context of the firm's culture. As discussed in Chapter 9, this requires careful attention to critical design elements that can more appropriately structure the PA event.

Many managers and researchers have downplayed the importance of performance appraisal. Current research, however, indicates that

PA need not be demotivational and, in fact, may contribute to goal attainment. When PA fails for professionals, it is typically because of a breakdown in the organizational systems that define, measure, reward, and give feedback on performance. These problems may be identified by critically diagnosing the organizational reward system.

Reward system diagnosis is an extremely important component of this book. The diagnostic activities, questions, and tests presented in Chapters 6 and 8 represent over a decade of applied research on organizational reward systems; they should be carefully considered when questions of attraction, motivation, and retention arise. Many of the problems associated with improving the performance of professionals and high-tech workers may be traced to breakdowns in the firm's reward structures and strategies. The culture of the firm plays an imposing role as well.

MANAGEMENT OF THE ORGANIZATION'S CULTURE

The 1980s have seen tremendous emphasis placed on designing and transforming a firm's culture. America has been fascinated with the examination of "culture" and has sought insights from foreign organizational cultures in an effort to isolate the organizational forms that either facilitate or hinder a firm's performance.

When we consider that we are in a crisis of economic productivity, the systematic investigation and dissection of culture has promised economic relief. That promise has not generally been kept; however, the study of culture has shed light on situational ingredients that affect performance. We know that some firms demand a high level of performance from their professional and high-tech workers. That demand can be exciting and challenging for some of the workers in that environment, but it can be debilitating as well. Other high-tech firms resemble "mom-and-pop" companies, with an emphasis more on "family" than on productivity. Each company culture has different HR practices, but none are quite so distinct as the organizational reward systems.

It is the contention here that a given company culture is best supported by integrating HR systems with the culture. This requires determining the fit between different HR practices and the culture of the firm. Most managers seem keen on enhancing creativity and innovations, yet disagree or are unclear on how to achieve this through culture change. To change a firm's culture, or to galvanize workers to achieve excellence, requires systematic consideration of what the desired goals are and an analysis of the HR practices that contribute to or detract from those goals.

Riggs (1983) suggests that the message must be clear as to what the vision of the new culture will be. For example, to stimulate a new product attitude, the message to professionals that new products will be marketed in a steady stream must be clearly stated. In that way, the absence of new products will be understood as the exception to the rule. That attitude must then be reinforced by the design of the reward system. Risk-taking should not be punished, particularly if it results in failure. An engineer managing a group of high-tech and professional employees once said, "If you're not failing, you're not taking risks. If you're not taking risks, then you're not going to be successful in this field."

Attention should be paid to articulating and communicating the vision of the desired culture. Further, systems must be established that reinforce the achievement of goals judged important to the new culture. Those systems involve not only human-resource practices but other structural systems that will enhance productivity.

STRUCTURAL ACCOMMODATIONS

Since high-tech firms are frequently on the cutting edge of new technologies, it is not surprising that scientists and engineers are now as important as key executives are to traditional firms (Gomez-Mejia and Balkin 1985). These industries are generally characterized by frequent changes, rapid innovations, short product life cycles, and rapid new product developments. They are also known to make quick changes in their work force, their organizational structure, and their operating procedures (Schoonhoven 1986). They are characterized by a very rapid rate and pace of change.

Equally characteristic of high-tech firms are their flexibility, their ability to retain an aura of entrepreneurialism, and their organization. These firms are fluid and flexible enough to adjust to the enormous number of changes in the external environment.

The messages of the 1960s and 1970s have supported organic structures as the best form for accommodating environmental uncertainty. These messages, however, have been questioned recently;

in fact, they have been proven unreliable in view of the swift technological changes that are now quite common to these industries. Unlike traditional firms, which encounter turbulence in their environment in terms of a few products or processes, high-tech firms live in a world of change. As such, the prescription for organic structures is insufficient.

The best-performing firms typically go through a period immediately after start-up when they tend to be flexible and adaptive; however, as they grow, it is critical that they develop clear, reproducible structures, even though a certain amount of structural inertia may thus be institutionalized. This is offset by frequent reorganizations, multiple roles, temporary teams and assignments, and coordination mechanisms based on frequent communications.

High-tech firms also make frequent use of project teams and task forces and have a sparse staff function. Generally, most high-tech firms are constructed along some type of matrix design that allows them to respond quickly to change. They also have small "garage"-type or intrapreneurial units that allow flexibility and adaptability as the firm grows in size. The key managerial challenge here is to integrate these various groups within the firm and to be able to change in response to any shift in strategy.

The control systems of high-tech firms resemble collegial control more than standardized control systems. There now is evidence that the more successful high-tech firms follow rational planning processes, even before the actual founding of the firm. Most successful high-tech firms are also fairly decentralized and have reward systems and other HR systems that are matched with the firm's culture.

When taken as a whole, the structure of the high-tech firm has a chameleon-like quality to it. Successful high-tech firms manage the process of constant change by altering their structures accordingly. They are simultaneously flexible and predictable in their HR practices. They manage the process of new product development and manufacturing with continuity and control, yet they reorganize these processes regularly. They may have a dual ladder to emphasize the importance of the technical experts, or they may even have a triple hierarchy that eases the tension between managers and professionals over resource allocation.

To prepare for the frequent changes, the high-tech firm must have a planning process that is linked directly to its business strategy and, where such exists, to its technology strategy.

FITNESS FOR FUTURE ACTION

A major challenge facing high-technology firms now and in the future will be developing even greater capacity to meet new challenges. As such, a certain amount of slack is needed in most systems. Further, there needs to be some balance between short-term and long-term priorities. American industry is fond of the bottom-line, which is generally based on short-term performance. We have seen that an overemphasis on the short term can mortgage the future and reduce the likelihood that a firm will be prepared for competition or innovation over the long haul.

Thus, it is imperative that the high-tech firm concentrate its energies on long-term priorities, in addition to demanding short-term results.

In conclusion, managers and the high-tech firms they work for would be well advised to bolster their capacity to meet new challenges in the following ways:

1. *They should recognize that managing high-technology and professional employees is significantly different from managing nonprofessionals.* This is true, in part, because professionals have a different set of values and characteristics, which have been gained through their socialization in the technical specialty. Managers need to be cognizant of those values and characteristics if they are to anticipate tension points and enhance the fit between the individual and the job.

2. *Managers should recognize that a certain amount of conflict will almost always exist between professionals and hierarchical authority and control systems.* The key is to transform this conflict into motivation by structurally insulating these workers from organizational pressures, while simultaneously making them aware of the importance that their work holds for the firm's well-being and its continued competitive advantage.

3. *They should attempt to develop HR practices and policies that have had some success in attracting, motivating, and retaining the high-tech work force.* That requires, at a minimum, knowledge of or systematic diagnosis of organizational practices, and matching the HR practices to the organization's culture. It also requires that a cadre of competent HR managers manage the transition. The days of

"ready-fire-aim" are over for high-technology firms seeking competitive advantage in their markets.

4. They should articulate the leader's vision, clearly establish the firm's goals, and ensure that all relevant parties are exposed to that thinking.

5. They should design jobs and work relationships to take advantage of technical specialties. For example, rotating professionals through multiple roles and job responsibilities can sensitize them to new ideas and opportunities.

6. They should establish career-sensitive tracking systems so that career development becomes an integrated part of their firms' practices.

7. They should utilize a menu of salient rewards that are relevant for high-tech and professional workers. These rewards ideally should be linked to performance, but in some cultures they might be linked to effort, risk-taking, or other relevant behaviors.

8. They should study the change process and learn from their experiences. High-tech firms change owing to internal and external factors, including departures from tradition, new leaders with new visions, crises or other startling events, key decisions on the part of senior management, or tests of their infrastructural ability to accommodate change. Firms also change because of change. But professionals and other high-tech workers must clearly see the need for change; otherwise, they may not support the change, or they may even sabotage it. Therefore, communication must be reemphasized.

In conclusion, this book has explored the major issues surrounding the management of high-technology and professional workers. Just as it is difficult to describe a prototypical high-tech or professional worker, so is it difficult to describe the typical high-tech firm. Each firm has a different company culture, and how each firm will respond to the suggestions in this book will undoubtedly vary.

It is fairly clear that there are fundamental differences between high-tech firms and more traditional manufacturing firms. High-tech firms tend to be more fluid and therefore more open to experimentation in their human-resource practices (Kleingartner and Anderson 1987). They also tend to be structured differently to accommodate changes. Their success is contingent upon the extent to which they can continuously innovate and design marketable products. This in turn is contingent upon their having the best human talent. We have established that attracting, motivating, and retaining this talent calls for innovative human-resource practices. These practices are best exercised when the firm's reward system is in sync with its culture.

This book should prove most useful to managers and researchers trying to assess the fit between the various components of a high-tech firm and the professionals who work in it. As such, this book should be used as a tool to begin diagnosing, assessing, and researching the effectiveness of the strategies and practices of those firms that are willing and able to meet the challenges in high tech's future.

REFERENCES

Arnold, Hugh, and Daniel C. Feldman. 1986. *Organizational Behavior.* New York: McGraw-Hill.

Bahrami, Homa, and Stuart Evans. 1987. "Stratocracy in High Technology Firms." *California Management Review* 30, no. 1 (Fall): 51–66.

Bailyn, Lotte. 1985. "Autonomy in the Industrial R&D Lab." *Human Resource Management* 24, no. 2 (Summer): 129–146.

_____ . 1982. "Resolving Contradictions in Technical Careers, or, What if I Like Being an Engineer?" *Technology Review* (November–December): 41–47.

Bailyn, Lotte, and John T. Lynch. 1983. "Engineering as a Life-Long Career: Its Meaning, Its Satisfactions, Its Difficulties." *Journal of Occupational Behavior* 4: 263–283.

Bayroff, A.G., H.R. Haggerty, and E.A. Rundquist. 1954. "Validity of Ratings as Related to Rating Techniques and Conditions." *Personnel Psychology* 7: 92–113.

Beer, Michael. 1981. "Performance Appraisal: Dilemmas and Possibilities." *Organizational Dynamics* (Winter): 24–36.

Bell, Daniel. 1976. "Conversation with Daniel Bell." *Organizational Dynamics*: 34–49.

Belous, Richard. 1987. "High Technology Labor Markets: Projections and Policy Implications." In *Human Resource Management in High Technology Firms*, edited by Archie Kleingartner and Carolyn Anderson, pp. 25–45. Lexington, Mass.: Lexington Books.

_____ . 1985. *The Computer Revolution and the U.S. Labor Force.* Washington, D.C.: U.S. Library of Congress, Congressional Research Service.

Benveniste, Guy. 1987. *Professionalizing the Organization*. San Francisco: Jossey-Bass.

Birnbaum, Philip H. 1988. "Coping With Environmental and Market Forces Impacting High Technology Industry in the 1990s." Plenary address at the Conference on Managing the High Technology Firm, Boulder, Colorado, University of Boulder, January 13–15.

Bittner, Reign H. 1948. "Developing an Industrial Merit Rating Procedure." *Personnel Psychology* 1: 403–432.

Bourgeois, L. Jay, and Kathleen M. Eisenhardt. 1987. "Strategic Decision Processes in Silicon Valley: The Anatomy of the 'Living Dead,'" *California Management Review* 30, no. 1 (Fall): 143–159.

Burns, Tom, and G.M. Stalker. 1961. *The Management of Innovation*. London: Tavistock Institute.

Business Week. 1987. "Where the New Jobs Will Be." (August 10): 50.

_____. 1984. "RCA: Will It Ever Be a Top Performer?" (April 2): 52–62.

_____. 1983. "Emerson Electric: High Profits from Low Tech." (April 4): 58–62.

_____. 1982. "Can John Young Redesign Hewlett-Packard?" (December 6): 72–78.

_____. 1980. "Corporate Culture: The Hard-To-Change Values That Spell Success or Failure." (October 27): 148–160.

Chandler, Alfred D. 1962. *Strategy and Structure*. Cambridge, Mass.: MIT Press.

Connor, Patrick. 1984. "Professionals in Organizations: Some Research Suggestions." *IEEE Transactions on Engineering Management* (EM-31): 7–11.

Cummings, Larry L., and Donald P. Schwab. 1973. *Performance in Organizations: Determinants and Appraisal*. Glenview, Ill.: Scott, Foresman.

Deluca, Joel, Michael Kitson, and Kathy Morris. 1985. "Towards a Human Systems Approach to Performance Appraisal." Sun Company working paper (March).

DeVries, David, Ann Morrison, Sandra Shullman, and Michael Gerlach. 1986. *Performance Appraisal on the Line*. Greensboro, N.C.: Center for Creative Leadership Publication.

Dorfman, Nancy S. 1982. "Massachusetts' High Technology Boom in Perspective: An Investigation of Its Dimensions, Causes and the Role of New Firms." MIT Center for Policy Alternatives, CPA 82-2 (April): 17–20.

Dowd, J.J., and Jeffrey Sonnenfeld. 1984. "A Note on Career Programs in Industry." In *Managing Career Systems*, edited by Jeffrey Sonnenfeld, pp. 318–328. Homewood, Ill.: Irwin.

Driver, Michael J. "Careers: A Review of Personal and Organizational Research." *International Review of Industrial and Organizational Psychology*. In press.

Drucker, Peter F. 1988. "The Coming of the New Organization." *Harvard Business Review* (January–February): 45–53.

Duchin, Faye, and Daniel B. Szyld. 1984. *A Dynamic Input-Output Model with Assured Positive Output*. New York: New York University Institute for Economic Analysis.

Duke, Paul Jr. 1987. "Taking the Long View." *Wall Street Journal* (June 12).

Durkheim, Emile. 1952. *The Division of Labor in Society*. Glencoe, Ill.: Free Press.

Ellis, N. D. 1969. "The Occupation of Science." *Technology and Science* 5, no. 1: 33–41.

Feldman, Daniel C. 1988. *Managing Careers in Organizations*. Glenview, Ill.: Scott, Foresman.

Finkelstein, Joseph, and David Newman. 1984. "The Third Industrial Revolution: A Special Challenge to Managers." *Organizational Dynamics* 13, no. 1 (Summer): 53–65.

Fombrun, Charles J., and Robert L. Laud. 1983. "Strategic Issues in Performance Appraisal: Theory and Practice." *Personnel* (November–December): 23–31.

Freeman, John, Glenn R. Carroll, and Michael T. Hannan. 1983. "The Liability of Newness: Age Dependence in Organizational Death Rates." *American Sociological Review* 48, no. 5 (October): 692–710.

Freidson, Eliott. 1970. *Professions of Medicine: A Study of the Sociology of Applied Knowledge*. New York: Dodd Mead.

Friar, John, and Mel Horwitch. 1985. "The Emergence of Technology Strategy: A New Dimension of Strategic Management." *Technology in Society* 7: 143–178.

Galbraith, Jay. 1977. *Organization Design*. Reading, Mass.: Addison-Wesley.

Gerpott, Torsten J., and Michel Domsch. 1985. "The Concept of Professionalism and the Management of Salaried Technical Professionals: A Cross-National Perspective." *Human Resource Management* 24, no. 2 (Summer): 207–226.

Gibson, Richard. 1987. "Managing the Techies." *Wall Street Journal* (June 12).

Gilb, C. 1966. *Hidden Hierarchies: The Professions and Government*. New York: Harper and Row.

Gomez-Mejia, Luis, and David Balkin. 1985. "Managing a High Tech Venture." *Organizational Dynamics* (February).

Gouldner, Alvin W. 1957. "Cosmopolitans and Locals—Toward an Analysis of Latent Social Roles I." *Administrative Science Quarterly* 2 (December): 281–306.

Greller, M. M., and David M. Herold. 1975. "Sources of Feedback: A Preliminary Investigation." *Organizational Behavior and Human Performance* 13: 244–256.

Griggs, Walter H., and Susan Manring. 1986. "Increasing the Effectiveness of Technical Professionals." *Management Review* (May): 62–64.

Grove, Andrew. 1983. *High Output Management*. New York: Random House.

Hall, Douglas T. 1976. *Careers in Organizations.* Pacific Palisades, Calif.: Goodyear Publishing.

Hall, Richard. 1968. "Professionalization and Bureaucratization." *American Sociological Review* 33 (February): 92–100.

Hallenberg, Edward X. 1970. "Dual Advancement Ladder Provides Unique Recognition for the Scientist." *Research Management* 13 (May): 221–227.

Hamilton, William F. 1985. "Corporate Strategies for Managing Emerging Technologies." *Technology in Society* 7: 197–212.

Hannan, Michael T., and John Freeman. 1984. "Structural Inertia and Organizational Change." *American Sociological Review* 49 (April): 149–164.

Hay Associates. 1985. "Survey of Incentive Practices in High Technology Firms." *Ideals and Trends.* Chicago: Commerce Clearing House.

Healey, Frank. 1960. "Job Status for the Research Scientist." *Research Management* 3 (Winter): 239–244.

Hower, Ralph, and Charles D. Orth. 1963. *Managers and Scientists.* Boston: Division of Research, Harvard Graduate School of Business Administration.

Hughes, Everett. 1958. *Men and Their Work.* Glencoe, Ill.: Free Press.

Ilgen, Dan, Cynthia Fisher, and M. S. Taylor. 1979. "Consequences of Individual Feedback on Behavior in Organizations." *Journal of Applied Psychology* 4: 349–371.

Ilgen, Dan, Terrence R. Mitchell, and James W. Fredrickson. 1981. "Poor Performers: Supervisors and Subordinates' Responses." *Organizational Behavior and Human Performance* 27: 386–440.

Ilgen, Daniel R., and Janet L. Barnes-Farrell. 1984. *Performance Planning and Evaluation.* Chicago: Science Research Associates Monograph.

Jackall, Robert, and Henry M. Levine. 1984. *Worker Cooperatives in America.* Berkeley: University of California Press.

Jansen, Erik. 1987. "Toward a Strategic Theory of Reward Systems." Ph.D. dissertation, University of Southern California.

Jansen, Erik, and Mary Ann Von Glinow. 1985. "Ethical Ambivalence and Organizational Reward Systems." *Academy of Management Review* 10, no. 4 (October): 814–822.

Johnson, Terence J. 1977. "The Professions in the Class Structure." In *Industrial Society: Class, Cleavage, and Control,* edited by R. Scase, New York: St. Martin's Press.

_____. 1972. *Professions and Power.* London: Macmillan Press.

Kanter, Rosabeth M. 1984. "Variations in Managerial Career Structures in High Technology Firms: The Impact of Organizational Characteristics on Internal Labor Market Patterns." In *Internal Labor Markets,* edited by Paul Osterman, pp. 109–131. Cambridge, Mass.: MIT Press.

_____. 1983. *The Change Masters.* New York: Simon and Schuster.

Kelley, Robert E. 1985. *The Gold Collar Worker: Harnessing the Brainpower of the New Workforce.* Reading, Mass.: Addison-Wesley.

Kerr, Jeffrey. 1984. "Diversification Strategies and Managerial Rewards: An Empirical Study." Working paper, School of Business, Southern Methodist University.

Kerr, Jeffrey, and John Slocum. 1987. "Managing Corporate Culture Through Reward Systems." *Academy of Management Executive* 1, no. 2 (May): 99–108.

Kerr, Steven. 1988. "Some Characteristics and Consequences of Organizational Reward Systems." In *Facilitating Work Effectiveness: Concepts and Procedures*, edited by David Schoorman and Benjamin Schneider, pp. 43–76. Lexington, Mass.: Lexington Books.

_____. 1975. "On the Folly of Rewarding A While Hoping for B." *Academy of Management Journal* 18, no. 4 (December): 769–783.

Kerr, Steven, and John Jermier. 1978. "Substitutes for Leadership: Their Meaning and Measurement." *Organizational Behavior and Human Performance* 22: 375–403.

Kerr, Steven, and John Slocum. 1981. "Controlling the Performances of People in Organizations." In *Handbook of Organizational Design*, edited by William Starbuck and Paul Nystrom, pp. 116–134. London: Oxford.

Kerr, Steven, Mary Ann Von Glinow, and Janet Schriesheim. 1977. "Issues in the Study of Professionals in Organizations: The Case of Scientists and Engineers." *Organizational Behavior and Human Performance* 18: 329–345.

Kilmann, Ralph. 1982. "Getting Control of the Corporate Culture." *Managing* 3: 11–17.

Klegon, Douglas. 1978. "The Sociology of Professions: An Emerging Perspective." *Sociology of Work and Occupations* 5, no. 3 (August): 257–283.

Kleingartner, Archie, and Carolyn Anderson. 1987. *Human Resource Management in High Technology Firms.* Lexington, Mass.: Lexington Books.

Kornhauser, William. 1962. *Scientists in Industry: Conflict and Accommodation.* Berkeley: University of California Press.

Landy, F. J., and J. L. Farr. 1980. "Performance Rating." *Psychological Bulletin* 87, no. 1: 72–107.

Latham, Gary, and Kenneth Wexley. 1981. *Increasing Productivity through Performance Appraisal.* Reading, Mass.: Addison Wesley.

Latham, Gary P., and Gary A. Yukl. 1975. "Assigned Versus Participative Goal Setting with Educated and Uneducated Woods Workers." *Journal of Applied Psychology* 60: 299–302.

Lawler, Edward E. 1984. "The New Pay." Working paper, Center for Effective Organizations, University of Southern California.

_____. 1983. "The Design of Effective Reward Systems." Working paper, Center for Effective Organizations, University of Southern California.

_____. 1971. *Pay and Organizational Effectiveness: A Psychological View.* New York: McGraw-Hill.

Lawrence, Paul H., and Jay W. Lorsch. 1969. *Organization and Environment: Managing Differentiation and Integration.* Homewood, Ill.: Irwin.

Lee, Sang. 1969. "Organizational Identification of Scientists." *Academy of Management Journal* 12, no. 3 (September): 327–337.

Leontief, Wassily, and Faye Duchin. 1984. *The Impact of Automation on Employment, 1963–2000.* New York: New York University Institute for Economic Analysis.

Leskin, Barry, University of Southern California Executive-in-Residence and Director of the Executive MBA Masters of Business Administration Conversation with the author, 1986.

_____ . Conversation with the author, 1984.

Lewin, Kurt. 1951. *Field Theory and Social Science.* New York: Harper Bros.

Madique, Modesto A., and Robert H. Hayes. 1984. "The Art of High Technology Management." *Sloan Management Review* 25, no. 2 (Winter): 17–31.

Mandt, Edward. 1978. "Managing Knowledge Workers." *Personnel Journal* (March): 138–143, 162.

Metzger, Robert O., and Mary Ann Von Glinow. "Off-Site Workers: At Home and Abroad." *California Management Review.* In press.

Miljus, Robert C., and Rebecca L. Smith. 1987. "Key Human Resource Issues for Management in High Tech Firms." In *Human Resource Management in High Technology Firms*, edited by Archie Kleingartner and Carolyn Anderson, pp. 115–131. Lexington, Mass.: Lexington Books.

Milkovich, George T. 1987. "Compensation Systems in High Technology Companies." In *Human Resource Management in High Technology Firms*, edited by Archie Kleingartner and Carolyn Anderson, pp. 103–114. Lexington, Mass.: Lexington Books.

Miller, Donald B. 1986. *Managing Professionals in Research and Development.* San Francisco: Jossey-Bass.

_____ . 1978. "Career Planning and Management in Organizations." In *Career Management for the Individual and the Organization*, edited by Marianne Jelinek, pp. 353–360. Chicago, Ill.: St. Clair Press.

Mills, Peter K., and James H. Morris. 1986. "Clients as 'Partial' Employees of Service Organizations: Role Development in Client Participation." *Academy of Management Review* 11, no. 4 (October): 726–735.

Mitchell, Graham R. 1985. "New Approaches for the Strategic Management of Technology." *Technology in Society* 7: 227–239.

Mohrman, Alan M. 1981. "Formal Performance Appraisal as an Intervention for the Integration of Performance and Quality of Worklife." Technical report T81-9 (15), Center for Effective Organizations, University of Southern California.

Morgan, Marilyn, Douglas T. Hall, and Ann Martier. 1979. "Career Development Strategies in Industry: Where Are We and Where Should We Be?" *Personnel* 56, no. 2: 13–30.

Morrison, Ann, Morgan McCall, and David DeVries. 1978, "Feedback to Managers: A Comprehensive Review of Twenty-four Instruments." Technical report no. 8, Center for Creative Leadership, Greensboro, North Carolina.

Morrison, Edward. 1987. "A Contingency Approach to Managing the High Tech Firm." Paper presented at the Western Academy of Management, Los Angeles, California, April 9–11.

Newman, John E., and John R. Hinrichs. 1980. *Performance Evaluation for Professional Personnel.* Scarsdale, N.Y.: Work in America Institute.

Patten, T. H., Jr. 1977. *Pay: Employee Compensation and Incentive Plans.* New York: Free Press.

Peters, Thomas J., and R. H. Waterman. 1982. *In Search of Excellence: Lessons from America's Best-Run Companies.* New York: Harper and Row.

Presthus, Robert. 1978. *The Organizational Society.* New York: St. Martin's Press.

Raelin, Joseph. 1987. "Two-Track Plans for One Track Careers." *Personnel Journal* 66, no. 1 (January): 96–101.

_____. 1985a. "The Basis for the Professional's Resistance to Managerial Control." *Human Resource Management* 24, no. 2 (Summer): 147–176.

_____. 1985b. *Clash of Cultures.* Boston: Harvard Business School Press.

Raelin, Joseph, C. K. Sholl, and D. Leonard. 1985. "Why Professionals Turn Sour and What to Do." *Personnel* 62, no. 10 (October): 28–41.

Reibstein, Larry. 1987. "More Employers Link Incentives to Unit Results." *Wall Street Journal* (April 10).

Resnick, Susan, and Alan M. Mohrman. 1982. "The Design of Performance Appraisal Systems: Some Implications From Research Findings." Technical report G82-5 (24), Center for Effective Organizations, University of Southern California.

Riche, Richard W., Daniel E. Hecker, and John U. Burgan. 1983. "High Technology Today and Tomorrow: A Small Slice of the Employment Pie." *Monthly Labor Review* (November): 50–58.

Riggs, Henry E. 1983. *Managing High-Technology Companies.* Belmont, Calif.: Lifetime Learning Publications.

Ritzer, George. 1972. *Man and His Work: Conflict and Change.* New York: Meredith Corporation.

Rogers, Everett M., and Annie Chen. 1987. "Technology Transfer and the Technopolis." Proceedings of the Pan Pacific Conference, Taipei, Taiwan, May.

Rogers, Everett M., and J. K. Larsen. 1984. *Silicon Valley Fever: Growth of High Technology Culture.* New York: Basic Books.

Rogers, Everett M., and Thomas W. Valente. 1988. "Technology Transfer in High Technology Industries." Paper presented at the Second Annual International Business Education and Research Program (IBEAR) Research Conference, University of Southern California, April 7–9.

Rogers, Rolf E. 1981. *Corporate Strategy and Planning*. Columbus, Ohio: Grid Publishing.

Roman, Daniel E. 1980. *Science, Technology, and Innovation: A Systems Approach*. Columbus, Ohio: Grid Publishing.

Roth, J. A. 1974. "Professionalism: The Sociologist's Decoy." *Sociology of Work and Occupations* 1: 6–23.

Sacco, George, and William Knopka. 1983. "Restructuring the Dual Ladder at Goodyear." *Research Management* 26, no. 4 (July–August): 36–41.

Schein, Ed. 1983. "Corporate Culture: What It Is and How to Change It." Working paper ONR TR-26, Sloan School of Management, Massachusetts Institute of Technology.

Schoonhoven, Claudia B. 1986. "Organizational Adaptation Caused by Technological Change: Issues and Analysis." Paper presented at the Western Academy of Management, Los Angeles, California, March 20–22.

Schoonhoven, Claudia B., and Kathleen M. Eisenhardt. 1987. "Surviving the 'Liability of Newness': A Model for Successful Entrepreneurship in Technology-Based Ventures." Paper presented at the Academy of Management, New Orleans, Louisiana, August 10–12.

Schriesheim, Janet, Mary Ann Von Glinow, and Steven Kerr. 1977. "Professionals in Bureaucracies: A Structural Alternative." In *Prescriptive Models of Organizations*, edited by Paul Nystrom and William Starbuck, pp. 55–69. North-Holland TIMS Studies in the Managemenr Sciences, vol. 5. Amsterdam: North-Holland.

Schuster, Jay. 1984. *Management Compensation in High Technology Companies*. Lexington, Mass.: Lexington Books.

Schuster, Jay. 1985. "Compensation Plan Design." *Compensation Plans* (May).

Scott, Richard W. 1966. "Professionals in Bureaucracies—Areas of Conflict." In *Professionalization*, edited by Howard Vollmer and Donald Mills, pp. 265–275. Englewood Cliffs, N. J.: Prentice-Hall.

Secrist, Horace. 1960. "Motivating the Industrial Research Scientist." *Research Management* 3 (Spring): 57–64.

Sethia, Nirmal, and Mary Ann Von Glinow. 1985. "Arriving at Four Cultures by Managing the Reward System." In *Gaining Control of the Corporate Culture*, edited by Kilmann, Saxton, Serpa and Associates, pp. 400–420. San Francisco: Jossey-Bass.

———. 1984. "Congruence of Cultures and Reward Systems: A Key Managerial Challenge." Working paper, University of Southern California.

Sexton, Donald L. 1988. "Propensity for Change: A Prerequisite for Growth in High Technology Firms." Paper presented at the conference, "Managing the High Technology Firm," Boulder, Colorado, January 13–15.

Smith, Patricia C. 1976. "Behaviors, Results and Organizational Effectiveness: The Problem of Criteria." In *Handbook of Industrial and Organizational Psychology*, edited by Marvin Dunnette, pp. 745–776. Chicago: Rand-McNally.

Spratt, Michael, and Bernadette Steele. 1985. "Rewarding Key Contributors." *Compensation and Benefits Review* 17, no. 3 (July-August): 24-37.

Stinchcombe, Arthur L. 1965. "Organizations and Social Structure." In *Handbook of Organizations*, edited by James March, pp. 153-193. Chicago: Rand-McNally.

Stonich, Paul J. 1984. "The Performance Measurement and Reward System: Critical to Strategic Management." *Organizational Dynamics* (Winter): 45-57.

Taylor, Robert L. 1986. "The Impact of Organizational Change on the Technological Gatekeeper Role." *IEEE Transactions on Engineering Management* EM-33, no. 1: 12-16.

Van de Ven, Andrew. 1980. "Early Planning: Implementation and Performance in New Organizations." In *The Organizational Life Cycle*, edited by John R. Kimberly et al., pp. 83-133. San Francisco: Jossey-Bass.

Van de Ven, Andrew, R. Hudson, and D. M. Schroeder. 1984. "Designing New Business Start-ups: Entrepreneurial, Organizational and Ecological Considerations." *Journal of Management.*

Von Glinow, Mary Ann. "Performance Appraisal for Scientific and Technical Professionals." In *The Design of Management Performance Appraisal Systems*, edited by Edward Lawler, Susan Resnick-West, and Alan Mohrman. San Francisco: Jossey-Bass. In press.

_____. 1985. "Reward Strategies for Attracting, Evaluating, and Retaining Professionals." *Human Resource Management* 24, no. 2 (Summer): 191-206.

_____. 1983. "Incentives for Controlling the Performance of High Technology and Professional Employees." *IEEE Transactions on Systems, Man and Cybernetics* SMC-13, no. 1 (January-February): 70-74.

_____. 1978. "Patterns of Congruity and Incongruity in an Emerging Profession: A Framework for Analysis." Ph.D. dissertation, The Ohio State University.

Von Glinow, Mary Ann, Michael Driver, Kenneth Brousseau, and Bruce Prince. 1983. "The Design of a Career Oriented Human Resource System." *Academy of Management Review* 8, no. 1 (January): 23-32.

Von Glinow, Mary Ann, and Nirmal Sethia. 1983. "The Role of Feedback in the Creation of Useful Knowledge." In *Producing Useful Knowledge for Organizations*, edited by Ralph Kilmann et al., pp. 221-244. New York: Praeger.

Walker, James W., and Thomas G. Gutteridge. 1979. "Career Planning Practices: An AMA Survey Report." American Management Association.

Wexley, Kenneth N. 1979. "Performance Appraisal and Feedback." In *Organizational Behavior*, edited by Steven Kerr, pp. 241-259. Columbus, Ohio: Grid Publishing.

Zonana, V.F. 1984. "Stirring Giant: Bank of America, Seeking Turnaround, Seems to Gain Ground." *Wall Street Journal* (January 27).

NAME INDEX

SUBJECT INDEX

ABOUT THE AUTHOR

Mary Ann Von Glinow is an associate professor of management and organization at the University of Southern California's Graduate School of Business Administration, as well as a faculty research scholar. She has received grants from the Department of Education and the Office of Naval Research to conduct research in the People's Republic of China, Korea, and Japan. Dr. Von Glinow has served on the Board of Directors of ITT's Center for the Study of Ethics in the Professions and on the Board of Governors of the Academy of Management. She is the chair-elect for the O.B. Division of the Academy and serves on the Academy's International Task Force.

Dr. Von Glinow is a coauthor of *Managing Complexity in High Technology Industries, Systems and People* and the author of numerous articles that have appeared in professional journals including *Organizational Behavior and Human Performance, Human Resource Management, Management Science, Academy of Management Review, IEEE Transactions,* and *Journal of Business Research.* She received a B.A. in political science from Bradley University, an M.B.A. and an M.A. in public administration, and a Ph.D. in management science from The Ohio State University.